Essential PHP for
Web Professionals

ISBN 0-13-088903-2

9 780130 889034

90000

Other Books in the Series

- *Essential PHP for Web Professionals*
  Christopher Cosentino

- *Essential CSS & DHTML for Web Professionals*
  Dan Livingston and Micah Brown

- *Essential JavaScript™ for Web Professionals*
  Dan Barrett, Dan Livingston, and Micah Brown

- *Essential Perl 5 for Web Professionals*
  Micah Brown, Chris Bellow, and Dan Livingston

- *Essential Photoshop® for Web Professionals*
  Brad Eigen, Dan Livingston, and Micah Brown

Coming soon...

- *Essential ASP for Web Professionals*

- *Essential JSP for Web Professionals*

- *Essential Photoshop® 5.5 for Web Professionals*

- *Essential Analysis and Design for Web Professionals*

Essential PHP for Web Professionals

Christopher Cosentino

Micah Brown
Series Editor

Prentice Hall PTR
Upper Saddle River, NJ 07458
www.phptr.com

Library of Congress Cataloging-in-Publication Data

Cosentino, Christopher.
    Essential PHP for Web professionals / Christopher Cosentino.
        p. cm. — (Essential series)
    Includes bibliographical references and index.
    ISBN 0-13-088903-2
        1. PHP (Computer program language) 2. Web sites—Design. I. Title. II. PH/PTR
essential series.

QA76.73.P224 C68 2000
005.2'762—dc21

00-063687

Editorial/Production Supervision: Jan H. Schwartz
Acquisitions Editor: Karen McLean
Cover Design Director: Jerry Votta
Cover Designer: Nina Scuderi
Manufacturing Manager: Alexis Heydt
Marketing Manager: Kate Hargett
Editorial Assistant: Rick Winkler
Art Director: Gail Cocker-Bogusz
Series Interior Design: Meg VanArsdale

© 2001 Prentice Hall PTR
Prentice-Hall, Inc.
Upper Saddle River, NJ 07458

Prentice Hall books are widely used by corporations and government agencies for
training, marketing, and resale.

The publisher offers discounts on this book when ordered in bulk quantities.
For more information, contact: Corporate Sales Department, Phone: 800-382-3419;
Fax: 201-236-7141; E-mail: corpsales@prenhall.com; or write: Prentice Hall PTR,
Corp. Sales Dept., One Lake Street, Upper Saddle River, NJ 07458.

Printed in the United States of America

10 9 8 7 6 5 4 3 2 1

ISBN 0-13-088903-2

Prentice-Hall International (UK) Limited, London
Prentice-Hall of Australia Pty. Limited, Sydney
Prentice-Hall Canada Inc., Toronto
Prentice-Hall Hispanoamericana, S.A., Mexico
Prentice-Hall of India Private Limited, New Delhi
Prentice-Hall of Japan, Inc., Tokyo
Pearson Education Asia Pte. Ltd.
Editora Prentice-Hall do Brasil, Ltda., Rio de Janeiro

Contents

Introduction

◆ Who Should Read This Book?

This book is meant to be a quick introduction to the PHP programming language for Web developers with little or no programming experience. This book assumes you know your HTML; it does not dwell on HTML fundamentals. If you can handle coding a few pages of HTML in a run-of-the-mill text editor, and want to learn how to add server-side functionality to your site, then this book is for you.

If you want to learn how to make Web development tasks easier, then this book is for you. This book teaches you about templates that can greatly reduce your coding time for a Web site.

If you are sick and tired of thirty-line PERL programs just to send a simple email from a Web site, then this book is for you. This book shows how easy coding routine Web applications in PHP can be.

If you want to learn a great up-and-coming Web development language, then this book is for you. PHP is getting more popular by the minute, and now PHP4 works with most of the popular Web servers on the Internet.

◆ How This Book Is Laid Out

This book teaches you about PHP in bite-sized mouthfuls; be sure to swallow before proceeding to the next section. Each chapter builds upon principles learned from the preceding chapters, so it's probably smart to go through the book starting at the beginning.

Each chapter contains code examples, explanations, and mini-projects. Larger projects are spaced out in the book so that you can use your newfound knowledge to build some nice Web applications.

All of the examples in the book are located on the companion Web site at *http://www.phptr.com/essential*. You can download the scripts needed to follow along with the exercises, or you can type them in by hand.

◆ A Little Background on PHP

PHP was originally written by Rasmus Lerdorf to add some functionality that the Web server didn't offer to his personal Web page. Soon other people started asking him if they could use his program for their own Web sites. Soon after that, people started asking for more features, and to make a long story short, Rasmus, with the help of others, created a new programming language called PHP/FI.

PHP/FI, which stood for Personal Home Pages/Form Interpreter, was updated and rewritten by a team of programmers working around the globe and was released as PHP3. At some point during the development of PHP3, the team decided that Personal Home Pages wasn't such a good name for the language they were creating, so a vote was called and PHP was officially renamed *PHP Hypertext Preprocessor,* which is a recursive acronym like GNU (GNU's not UNIX).

PHP3 was also updated and worked on by the team of programmers, and PHP4 was created. PHP4 comes with a new *engine* called Zend. See *http://www.zend.com* for more information on Zend.

Both PHP3 and PHP4 are robust and versatile languages that, in my honest opinion, are easier to use, more powerful, and just cooler than most of the other offerings in the Web scripting language market.

◆ How PHP and HTML Work Together

PHP has advantages over other programming languages that are used for HTML processing in that it was designed specifically for one purpose, and that is to work with HTML. It comes to little surprise then that it works with HTML in such a simple, yet powerful, manner.

When a browser requests a PHP page from a Web server, the PHP module looks over the page (parses it) before sending it to the browser. The parts of the page that are written in normal HTML are sent to the browser just as they normally would be in a regular HTML document. The parts of it that are written in PHP are processed by the server's PHP module, which is the program that interprets the PHP code. The PHP module looks at the PHP code and executes the instructions it finds there. Those instructions tell the server to do things like send email, access a database, or crunch numbers.

◆ Notes About This Book and the Web Site

All of the code examples from this book are available for download on the book's Web site at *http://www.phptr.com/essential*. You can download it from the Web site or type it all in yourself. It's recommended you try typing it in so you can get used to the syntax and become familiar with the examples.

In addition to the code examples, the answers to the *Advanced Projects* from the end of each chapter are also included on the Web site. Play around with these to further develop your skills in coding PHP.

Also have a look at the other books in the series on the site. All of the books are excellent guides to their respective subjects.

There will also be updates posted on this site for any errata that may occur with the book. PHP is an evolving language and sometimes functions or code constructs change slightly as the language develops.

In this *Essential Web Professionals* series, we have created two fictitious companies that we feel portray a large percentage of the types of companies that are getting involved with exposure on the Web.

- *Stitch Magazine*: *Stitch* is an online fashion magazine that has chosen to publish parts of the magazine on the Web to complement its printed version. It's also using the Web to reach new readers.

- Shelley Biotechnologies: This is a company that sells biotech products and wishes to enter the online world to advertise them.

Although every company is different in its own way, we have found that most really do fall into one of these two categories.

◆ What This Book Will and Won't Teach You

PHP is a rich and full-featured language. A book this size couldn't possibly cover each and every function that's in PHP. This book is meant to get you started using the PHP language. It takes some of the more widely used techniques for Web development using PHP and breaks them into their basic parts. You can then use these parts in your own development projects.

After you've read through this book, you should have a very solid understanding of PHP and how it can help you accomplish your Web development tasks. Hopefully, this book will be a stepping stone for further studies and experiments in PHP.

Acknowledgments

I would like to thank my partner and the love of my life, Sarah, for the love and support she has shown throughout this endeavor and countless others. Thanks for your love and smiles, and for putting up with the endless hours I spend in front of the computer when I really should be spending that time with you.

Also, many thanks go out to my parents, Anthony and Dianne, and my brother, Patrick, for everything they've done for me throughout the years. Your love, guidance, and support have helped me achieve so many of my goals.

Thanks also go out to Micah Brown for giving me the opportunity to write this book and for his excellent support throughout the project.

About the Author

Christopher Cosentino has worked as a technical writer and Web developer at Lucent Technologies since 1995 and also as a freelance Web developer of small e-commerce sites since 1996. He specializes in PHP, PERL, and ASP programming, and Linux and Apache administration.

By the time Chris was 12, his talent for programming had set his career course. His computer science education and his natural curiosity about programming led him to explore various Web technologies, including PHP. Since he discovered how easy it is to use, he has used PHP on every site he has worked on—from e-commerce to custom project tracking tools.

1 Getting Started

IN THIS CHAPTER

- Introduction
- Installing Apache and PHP on Windows
- Installing Apache and PHP on Linux
- The php.ini File
- Comments in Scripts

◆ Introduction

Before you can start programming in PHP, you need to install the proper software. In this case, you need to install the Apache Web server and PHP. Installation is usually quick and painless. But, if you do run into problems, be sure to consult the documentation provided with the Apache and PHP programs.

◆ Installing Apache and PHP on Windows

These steps will guide you through setting up Apache and PHP on your Windows 95, 98, or NT system. First you need to set up Apache; then set up PHP.

To Install Apache

1. Point your Web browser at *http://www.apache.org/httpd. html.*
2. Click on the *Download* link.
3. Click on the *Binaries* link.
4. Click on the *Win32* link.
5. Many versions of the Apache Web server show up. Click on *apache_1_3_12_win32.exe* or a higher version. Be sure not to get an alpha version. You want to get the latest stable release.
6. A dialog box asking if you want to save the file should open in your browser. Save the file to your hard drive.
7. Go to the folder where you saved the Apache.exe file and double-click it. This runs the Apache Installer.
8. If prompted for a location to install the file, just choose the default location. Normally this is in C:\Program Files\Apache Group\Apache or something similar, depending on your version of Windows.
9. From the Windows Start Menu, select *Start → Program Files → Apache Web Server → Start Apache.*
10. A DOS window stating that Apache is running should appear. Don't close this window or Apache will stop running.
11. Open a browser and type in *http://localhost/* for the URL.
12. A page similar to the one in Figure 1–1 should appear in your browser.

To Install PHP

You need WinZip to open the files for PHP. If you don't have it, you can get it from *http://www.winzip.com.*

1. Point your browser at *http://www.php.net.*
2. Click on the *Download* link on the left-hand side of the page.
3. Click on the appropriate PHP file for Windows (you can grab the php3 file, the php4 file, or both) by clicking on it. PHP3 and PHP4 can both easily be installed on a Windows machine.
4. A dialog box asking if you want to save the file should open in your browser. Save the file to your hard drive.
5. Go to the folder where you saved the PHP.zip file and double-click it.

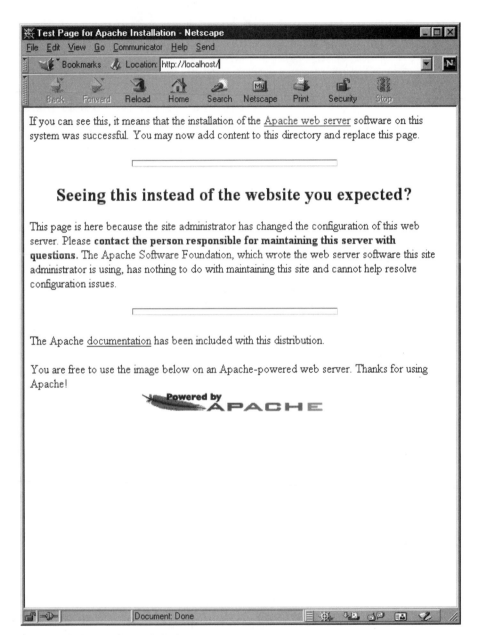

FIGURE 1-1 Apache on Windows

6. WinZip should open. Click on the *Extract* button and extract all the files in the zip file to a temporary folder.

7. Make sure your system is set to *Show All* files. There are .dll files included in the zip file that will be hidden if you have your system files hidden.

8. Copy all of the .dll files from the temporary folder where you extracted the PHP files, to your Windows systems folder. (On Windows 95/98 this is C:\windows\system. On Windows NT it is c:\WINNT\system.)

9. Rename the php3.ini-dist file (or php.ini-dist file if you are using PHP4) in the temporary directory to *php.ini* and copy it to your Windows directory (C:\windows or C:\WINNT, depending on your version of Windows).

10. Create a folder in C:\ called *php3* or *php4*, depending on the version you are using.

11. Copy php.exe into the php folder you just created.

12. Open the httpd.conf file in C:\Program Files\Apache Group\Apache\conf in a text editor. You can use any text editor to edit this file, but when you save the file be sure to save it as plain text and not as a .doc file or other format.

13. Add the following lines at the end of httpd.conf if you are using PHP4:

```
ScriptAlias /php4/ "C:/php4/"
AddType application/x-httpd-php .php
Action application/x-httpd-php "/php4/php.exe"
```

14. Add the following lines at the end of httpd.conf if you are using PHP3:

```
ScriptAlias /php3/ "C:/php3/"
AddType application/x-httpd-php3 .php3
Action application/x-httpd-php3 "/php3/php.exe"
```

15. If you are installing only PHP4, also add the following line:[1]

```
AddType application/x-httpd-php .php3
```

The line above allows the examples in this book to work correctly if only PHP4 is installed.

---

1. The *.php3* extension is traditionally reserved for PHP3 scripts. The *.php* extension is used for PHP4 files. The examples in this book all have a .php3 extension, but work equally well in PHP3 and PHP4. If you in-

16. Be sure to save the httpd.conf file.

17. Stop and start the Apache Web server using the Start Menu icons in the *Apache Web Server* folder. This causes Apache to reload its configure scripts and recognize that PHP functionality has been added.

18. Create a one-line PHP script in the C:\Program Files\ Apache Group\Apache\htdocs folder. You can use any text editor to create the script; just be sure to save the file with a *.php3* extension. The file should be named *info* *.php3*. The one line is

```
<? phpinfo(); ?>
```

19. Open your browser and point it at *localhost/info.php3*. You should get a page like the one in Figure 1–2. (If you installed PHP3, the page will look slightly different.)

If you are using Windows, then that's all there is to it for the installation stage. You can now start programming in PHP. But remember, whenever you want to run a script on your local machine, 1) have Apache running, and 2) place all of your files in the *htdocs* folder in the Apache installation. Whenever you want to access one of your scripts, you just need to point your browser at *localhost/Name_of_Script.php3*.

◆ Installing Apache and PHP on Linux

These steps will guide you through setting up Apache and PHP on your Linux box. First you need to set up Apache; then set up PHP.

To Install Apache

1. Download the source tarball from *www.apache.org/dist/*. It should be in the form of apache_VERSION.tar.gz, where VERSION is something like 1.3.12.

2. A dialog box asking if you want to save the file should open in your browser. Save the file to your hard drive.

3. Unzip the downloaded file with the command

```
gunzip apache_VERSION.tar.gz
```

---

stall only PHP4, then this additional line lets you run all the scripts in this book unmodified, but it probably wouldn't be a good idea to make this change on a production server.

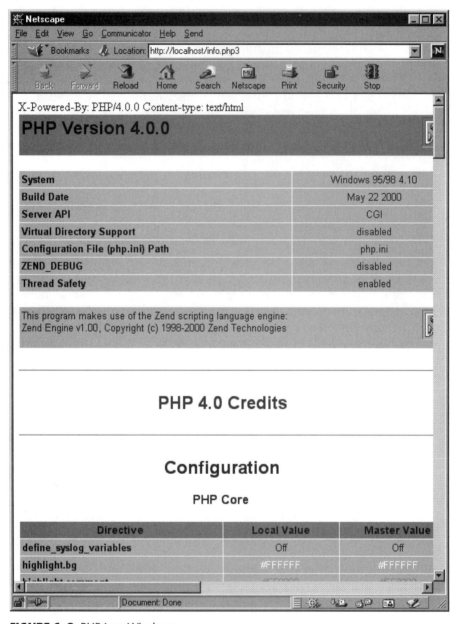

FIGURE 1–2 PHP4 on Windows

4. Untar the version with the command

```
tar -xvf apache_VERSION.tar
```

5. Change the directory to the newly created directory with the command

```
cd apache_VERSION
```

6. Run the configure script. I use the following options:

```
./configure --prefix=/usr/local/apache \
> --enable-module=most \
> --enable-shared=max
```

This places the Apache installation in the */usr/local/apache* directory and enables most of the built-in modules.

7. Once the configure script has finished running, issue the command

```
make
```

8. After the `make` command has finished, issue the command

```
make install
```

9. After the program has been installed, you may want to add a line to your init scripts so that Apache is restarted each time you reboot your system. To do this, add a line to your */etc/rc.d/rc.local* (or comparable file for your distro) that says

```
/usr/local/apache/apachetcl start
```

10. Test the installation by opening a browser and checking your local host (or the IP of your Linux machine if it's on a LAN). In my case, my Linux server is on my local LAN with an IP of 192.168.0.1.

11. A page similar to the one in Figure 1–1 should appear in your browser.

To Install PHP

1. Point your browser at *http://www.php.net*.

2. Click on the *Download* link on the left-hand side of the page.

3. Click on the appropriate PHP source tarball for Linux (you can grab the php3 file, the php4 file, or both) by clicking on it. At the time of this writing, PHP3 and PHP4 cannot easily be installed at the same time on a Linux box, but the PHP developers are said to be working on a resolution to this problem.

4. A dialog box asking if you want to save the file should open in your browser. Save the file to your hard drive.

5. After the file downloads, unzip the file with the command

```
gunzip php-4.0.0.tar.gz
```

(Be sure to replace the php-4.0.0.tar.gz filename with the name of the version that you downloaded.)

6. Untar the file with the command

```
tar -xvf php-4.0.0.tar
```

7. Change the directory to the php-4.0.0 directory and issue the configure command

```
/configure -with-apxs=/usr/local/apache/bin/apxs
```

8. Once the configure script has finished running, issue the command

```
make
```

9. After the `make` command has finished, issue the command

```
make install
```

10. Now open the *httpd.conf* file in C:\Program Files\Apache Group\Apache\conf in a text editor. You can use any text editor to edit this file, but when you save the file, be sure to save it as plain text and not as a .doc file or other format.

11. Add the following lines at the end of *httpd.conf* if you are using PHP4:

```
ScriptAlias /php4/ "C:/php4/"
AddType application/x-httpd-php .php
Action application/x-httpd-php "/php4/php.exe"
```

12. Add the following lines at the end of *httpd.conf* if you are using PHP3:

```
ScriptAlias /php3/ "C:/php3/"
AddType application/x-httpd-php3 .php3
Action application/x-httpd-php3 "/php3/php.exe"
```

13. If you are installing only PHP4, also add the following line:[2]

```
AddType application/x-httpd-php .php3
```

The line above allows the examples in this book to work correctly if only PHP4 is installed.

14. Be sure to save the *httpd.conf* file.

15. Stop and start the Apache Web server using the Start Menu icons in the *Apache Web Server* folder. This causes Apache to reload its configure scripts and recognize that PHP functionality has been added. You can do this by issuing the commands

```
/usr/local/apache/bin/apachectl stop
/usr/local/apache/bin/apachectl start
```

16. Create a one-line PHP script in the \usr\local\apache\htdocs directory. You can use any text editor to create the script; just be sure to save the file with a *.php3* extension. The file should be named *info.php3*. The one line is

```
<? phpinfo(); ?>
```

17. Open your browser and point it at *http://localhost/info.php3*. (or the IP of your Linux server if it is not a local installation). You should get a page that looks like Figure 1–2. (If you installed PHP3, the page will look slightly different.)

◆ The php.ini File

The *php.ini* file (or *php3.ini* if you are using PHP3) controls some of the default ways that PHP works. These settings can be changed according to your particular needs for PHP. The file contains PHP directives with corresponding values that can enable or disable the feature or set a certain value, such as link color.

To see a list of these values, you can just look at the little *info.php3* script you created to test the PHP installation.

---

2. The *.php3* extension is traditionally reserved for PHP3 scripts. The *.php* extension is used for PHP4 files. The examples in this book all have a *.php3* extension, but work equally well in PHP3 and PHP4. If you install only PHP4, then this additional line lets you run all the scripts in this book unmodified, but it probably wouldn't be a good idea to make this change on a production server.

The online PHP manual at *http://www.php.net* contains the specifics for each of the configurable options and the possible settings you can alter.

◆ Comments in Scripts

One final thing before you begin coding your PHP scripts: make sure you adequately comment your scripts! If you are unfamiliar with coding, now is the best time to instill some good coding habits. Comments in a script are like a help file for programmers working on someone else's code.

A comment, when embedded in PHP code, looks like this:

```
<?
/* This is a
   multi-line comment */
… some php code…
// This is a single line comment.
… some php code…
?>
```

A comment essentially explains what a code snippet is doing (or whatever you want it to say). This is especially useful if the code snippet is rather nonintuitive. Your comment can help other programmers understand what is happening at a particular point in the script, and also remind you, should you not happen to look at the script for a while, what you were doing at that point in the script.

The corresponding features in HTML are the `<!--` and `//-->` tags.

Additionally, you can use comments to block out portions of your script that you don't want to execute, just as you can in HTML with the above tags.

2 Your First Dynamic Web Pages

IN THIS CHAPTER

- New Functions
- Conventions in PHP
- Embedding PHP into Your HTML Pages
- Understanding Variables
- Using Data from a Form
- Passing Information through a Form and Links

◆ The Basics of Server-Side Scripting

Server-side scripting lets you enter a whole new world of Web site creation. No longer are you hindered by the static and noninteractive nature of plain HTML. This chapter familiarizes you with some of the ultra-basics of PHP. This chapter teaches you how to output text to a browser from the script, how variables work, and how to pass variables through a form or links on a page to a script.

◆ New Functions

print()

```
print( string );
```

The `print()` function is one of the most basic functions used in PHP. It allows you to send output from your script to the browser.

```
print("Welcome to the world of PHP.\n");
```

The above example simply prints out the sentence *Welcome to the world of PHP.* on a Web page. The \n at the end of the sentence tells PHP to insert a new line at the end of the sentence. This new line is viewable only in the source. It doesn't add a new line in the actual text displayed in the browser.

When sending text from your script to the browser, you need to remember that the browser interprets this text as HTML. A better example of using the `print()` function might be

```
print("<H1>Welcome to the world of PHP.</H1>\n<P>");
```

This example prints *Welcome to the World of PHP.* in the browser, but instead of formatting it as plain text, the browser formats it as Heading 1 text. If you viewed the source of this script in a browser, you would simply see

```
<H1>Welcome to the world of PHP.</H1>
<P>
```

More information about the `print()` function is available in the online version of the PHP manual at *http://www.php.net/manual/function.print.php3.*

◆ Conventions in PHP

There are a few simple conventions that you must use when programming in PHP. These conventions are standard rules that you need to apply to your script so that the Web server can correctly interpret your code. If you do not follow these basic rules, you'll encounter the ubiquitous *parse error.* Parse errors are a way of life for new PHP programmers. At one time or another, you'll forget to follow one of the basic rules and the script will bomb out on you with the message, "parse error on line 23," or a similar message. They are annoying, but usually easy to fix, especially once you know the basic rules.

PHP Start and End Tags

The most common convention that you need to follow is to enclose all of the PHP parts of your script within the PHP start and end tags. These tags are <?PHP and ?> respectively. These tags tell the Web server that anything contained within the tags is PHP code and should be interpreted as such. If your server is set up to use short tags, you can use <? and ?>.[1] Examples throughout this book use both methods.

Semicolons

The other fundamental rule that you need to follow is to place semicolons at the end of each line of PHP code. Note that this doesn't mean after each physical line, but after each command that you write.

```
print("This is a valid
    line of PHP code.\n");
```

The previous line command equals one valid line of code. The semicolon is placed at the end of the second physical line, indicating the end of the command.

There are some exceptions when you won't need to place a semicolon at the end of the line. These include

- If the line ends in a colon (:)
- If the line ends in an open ({) or close (})curly brace
- If the line ends with the open (<?) or close (?>) PHP tag

See the PHP manual at *http://www.php.net/manual/html/language.basic-syntax.html* for more information on basic conventions used in PHP.

◆ **Embedding PHP into Your HTML Pages**

Creating a site that uses PHP is almost the same as creating a site that uses plain old HTML. You can use one of many WYSIWYG[2] HTML editors, or you can use a text editor. The basic principles for coding PHP scripts are the same as for writing HTML; write your HTML and PHP markup, then test it in a browser.

When you are writing your PHP scripts, you must specify to the Web server which parts of the page the Web server needs to process using PHP and which parts of the page should be processed as normal HTML. When a Web server sends plain

---

1. See Chapter 1 for instructions on enabling the use of short tags and other server settings in the php.ini file.
2. What You See Is What You Get

HTML information to a browser, it just spits out the file without even really parsing (reading in) the content of the file. The Web server must parse PHP (read every line and process it), so you always need to specify when you are breaking out of HTML and going into PHP. Tagging the PHP parts of your page with PHP tags tells the Web server to start reading the files and parse them according to the PHP language. Anything between these tags is evaluated by the PHP part of the Web server.

The most basic example of this is

```
1. <html>
2. <head><title>The First Rule</title></head>
3. <body>
4. <?php
5. print("PHP stands for <b>PHP Hypertext Preprocessor\n</b>");
6. ?>
7. </body>
8. </html>
```

For the most part, this script looks like normal HTML markup, except for lines 4 through 6. If you were to view the script in a browser, it would look like Figure 2–1.

And if you were to look at the source code from within the browser you would simply see

```
<html>
<head><title>The First Rule</title></head>
<body>
PHP stands for <b>PHP Hypertext Preprocessor</b>
</body>
</html>
```

When the page is requested, the Web server processes the page as normal HTML until it encounters the <?php tag (in line 4 of the example). Once the Web server reaches line 4, it interprets the rest of the page as PHP, until it gets to a ?> tag (in line 6); at that point, the Web server returns to processing the page as normal HTML until it either gets to another <?php tag or the page ends.

You can go back and forth between PHP and HTML as often as you'd like within a single page. Just be sure to include all the opening and closing PHP tags. The Web server needs to do additional processing when interpreting PHP, so it's actually more efficient for the server to serve static HTML rather than process PHP. Try to keep the parts of your pages that remain static out of the PHP processor.

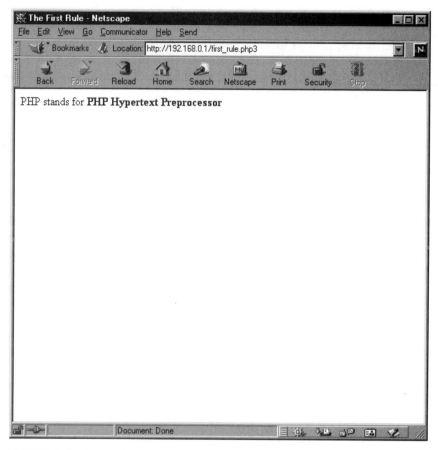

FIGURE 2-1 Output from the print() function

You could have a script like the one below, which is parsed by the Web server entirely as PHP.

```
<?php
print("<html>\n");
print("<head>\n");
print("<title>An Inefficient Script</title>\n");
print("</head>\n");
print("<body>\n");
print("<p>This script could be better written in HTML\n");
print("<p>It's just wasting server resources\n");
print("</body>\n");
print("</html\n");
?>
```

The script above is just plain useless when written in PHP. It's the perfect example of what *not* to do when writing your PHP scripts. Although this is a simple example, it shows that PHP can produce static pages just as HTML can. But it requires more work for you to write the script, and it requires more work for the Web server to dole out the page to a browser.

An inherently nondynamic page won't suddenly become dynamic just because you used PHP to print static lines of text to the browser.

◆ Understanding Variables

At this point, it doesn't look like PHP can do much more than plain old HTML. It can print text to a browser. Big deal. But let's introduce one of the core building blocks of any programming language—variables.

The easiest way to think about a variable is to think of it as a container, such as a piece of Tupperware. With a piece of Tupperware, you can store things such as leftover meatloaf, a sandwich, or maybe some potato chips. But the real value of Tupperware is that you can use it for meatloaf one day, then take out the meatloaf and put in your sandwich the next day, over and over again with many different types of foods. And in theory, Tupperware is supposed to preserve the food in the same state as when you put the food in it (for a short time at least, but don't worry—the contents of your variables won't mold in PHP).

Variables in PHP are much the same as Tupperware. One moment they can store a string such as *Meatloaf,* and the next moment they can store a string such as *Sandwich.* Even better than that, variables in PHP can store any kind of value, such as a string, integer, or decimal number.[3] There are even variables in PHP, called *arrays,* that store multiple values, which are like multi-compartment pieces of Tupperware. Arrays are introduced in Chapter 3, "User Interaction: PHP With Forms and Cookies."

Variables in PHP must have a $ in front of their names. If you had a variable called *Tupperware,* and you wanted to store the string *Meatloaf* in that variable, you'd put it into your PHP script like this:

---

3. Numbers with decimals in them, such as 3.14, are also referred to as *floating point* numbers in programming-speak.

```
$tupperware = "Meatloaf";
```

The equal sign(=) assigns the string to the variable.

To use the newly created variable in your script, you could do something like this:

```
print("For leftovers we have some $tupperware\n.");
```

When that line is viewed in a browser, it is displayed like this:

```
For leftovers we have some Meatloaf.
```

More information about variables is available in the PHP manual at *http://www.php.net/manual/html/language.variables.html*.

Now let's use the variable the way it is supposed to be used, with *variable* information.

Script 2-1 shows how the same variable, $tupperware, can store different information throughout the script.

Figure 2–2 illustrates the screen result of Script 2-1.

Script 2-1
variables.php3

```
 1. <html>
 2. <head>
 3. <title>Using Variables in PHP--Tupperware Example</title>
 4. </head>
 5. <body bgcolor="#FFFFFF">
 6. <?php
 7. $tupperware = "Meatloaf";
 8. print ("<p>On Monday we had $tupperware for leftovers.\n");
 9. $tupperware = "Chicken Parmesan";
10. print ("<p>On Tuesday we had $tupperware for leftovers.\n");
11. $tupperware = "Steak Tips";
12. print ("<p>On Wednesday we had $tupperware for leftovers.\n");
13. ?>
14. </body>
15. </html>
```

HOW THE SCRIPT WORKS

- Lines 1 through 5 are plain HTML.
- Line 6 is the opening PHP tag. It tells the Web server to start processing the script as PHP, and not as HTML.
- Line 7 assigns a value to the variable; the script is storing your string in the variable. In this case, the variable $tupperware is being assigned the value *Meatloaf.*

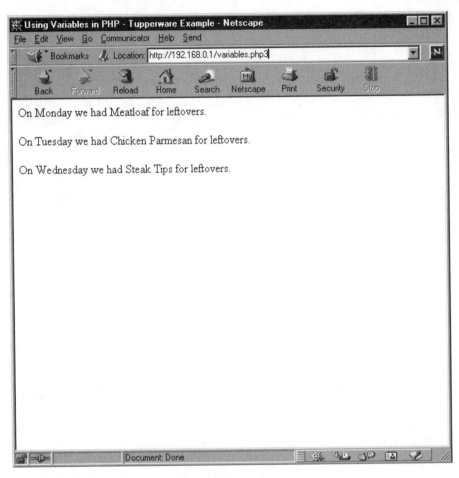

FIGURE 2-2 Output from variables.php3

- Line 8 prints the sentence to the browser. The variable name `$tupperware` is not printed to the browser; instead, its content (value) is.
- Lines 9 and 10 are the same as lines 7 and 8, but the day and type of leftover are changed.
- Lines 11 and 12 are the same as above. New day, new leftover.
- Line 13 is the end PHP tag. It tells the Web server to stop processing the page as PHP and start processing the page as normal HTML again.
- Lines 14 and 15 are normal HTML that close the page.

◆ Using Data from a Form

So you have the ability to print output to the browser and use variables to store some information. How is this useful? The real usefulness of this comes when you use your newfound knowledge with a form. With PHP, you can take any and all input filled in by a user via a form and store all of that information in variables. Then, as you'll learn in later chapters, you can take that information and store it in a database or to a file.

When creating your forms in HTML, you need to name the elements of the form. For example, if you have a form asking a user for information, and you want to ask the user's first name, you can create the HTML like this:

```
<form action=first_name.php3">
<p>First Name: <input type="text" name="first_name">
<input type="submit" name="submit">
</form>
```

You cannot have any spaces in the names of the input fields in the form. The name of the input field will be the name of the variable when you send the results of a form to a PHP script, and variable names can't have spaces in them.

You can use the input from the form in your script once the form has been filled in and the user hits the Submit button.

In the above example you would access the variable just by adding a $ in front of the input name. For example,

```
print("Hello $first_name!\n");
```

This line prints out the name entered into the form by the user.

Scripts 2-2 and 2-3 show how to get some basic contact information from a form, then use the resulting variables to create a dynamically generated page. The first script is really just an HTML page, and everything in it should look pretty familiar to you. The second script is the actual PHP script that processes the information received from the first script.

The screen result of Script 2-2 is shown in Figure 2–3, and the screen result of Script 2-3 is shown in Figure 2–4.

Script 2-2
form_entry.html

```
1.  <html>
2.  <head>
```

```
 3. <title>Entering Information into a Form</title>
 4. </head>
 5. <form action="form_results.php3" method="GET">
 6. <p>First Name: <input type="text" name="first_name">
 7. <br>Last Name: <input type="text" name="last_name">
 8. <br>Address: <input type="text" name="address">
 9. <br>City: <input type="text" name="city">
10. <br>State: <input type="text" name="state">
11. <br>Zip: <input type="text" name="zip">
12. <br>Home Phone: <input type="text" name="home_phone">
13. <p><input type="submit" name="Submit">
14. <input type="Reset">
15. </form>
16. </body>
17. </html>
```

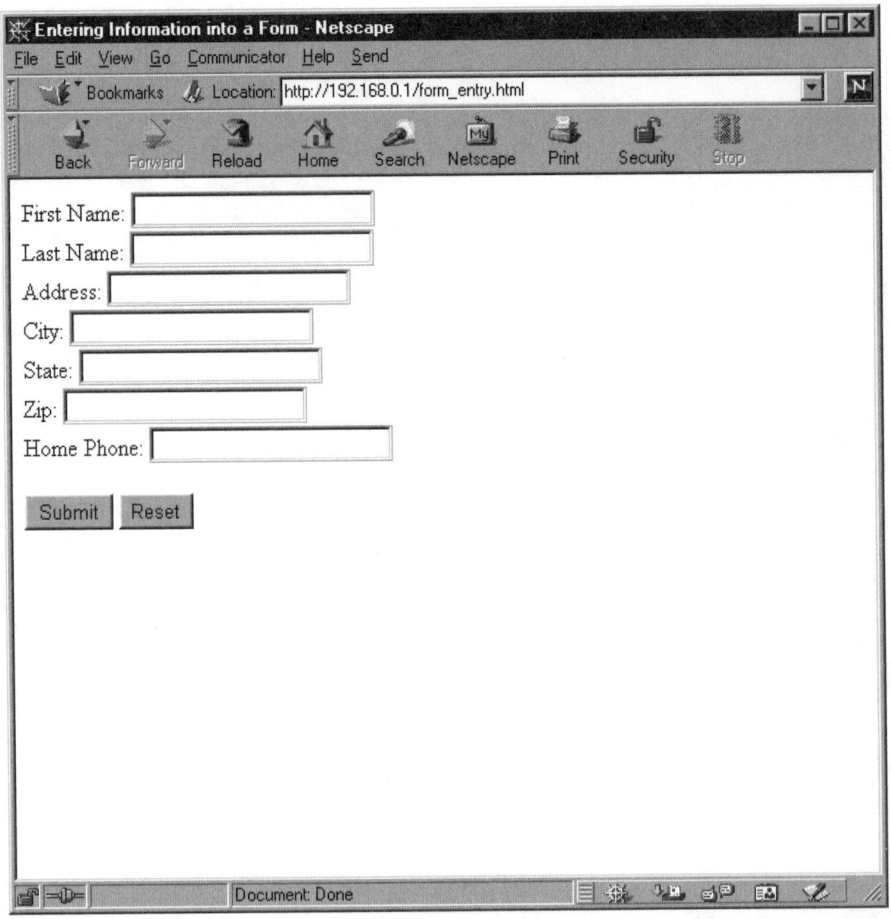

FIGURE 2–3 The form from form_entry.html

Script 2-3
form_results.php3

```
 1.  <html>
 2.  <head>
 3.  <title>Form Results</title>
 4.  </head>
 5.  <body>
 6.  <h2>Below are the results of your Form Submission</h2>
 7.  <?php
 8.  print("<p>First Name: <b>$first_name</b>\n");
 9.  print("<br>Last Name: <b>$last_name</b>\n");
10.  print("<br>Address: <b>$address</b>\n");
11.  print("<br>City: <b>$city</b>\n");
12.  print("<br>State: <b>$state</b>\n");
```

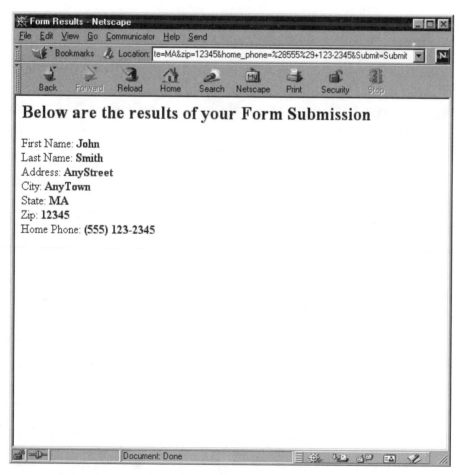

FIGURE 2–4 Output from form_results.php3

```
13. print("<br>Zip: <b>$zip</b>\n");
14. print("<br>Home Phone: <b>$home_phone</b>\n");
15. ?>
16. </body>
17. </html>
```

HOW THE SCRIPT WORKS

- Lines 1 through 6 are normal HTML.
- Line 7 is the opening PHP tag. It tells the Web server to start processing the script as PHP, and not as HTML.
- Lines 8 through 14 print out the information that the user entered into the form. Some basic HTML formatting is applied to distinguish the user-entered information from the rest of the page.
- Line 15 contains the end PHP tag. It tells the Web server to start processing the page as normal HTML again.
- Lines 16 and 17 close out the HTML for the page.

◆ Passing Information through a Form and Links

Now that you can get information from a user via a form and store that information in variables, you can begin to create some dynamic aspects of your site.

If you look at the URL in Figure 2–4, you'll see something like the following:

```
http://localhost/form_results.php3?first_name=John&last_name=...
```

All the items after the question mark (?) in the URL are variable names and values sent from the form to the server. This grouping is called name/value pairs. Each item has a variable name and a corresponding value, even if the value is null, or nothing. Each of the name/value pairs is separated by the ampersand symbol (&). You'll often notice this when submitting information from a form that is using the **GET** method. Forms that use the **POST** method do not print the variable names and values in the URL.

The ability to pass information from forms to the server is beneficial to PHP developers because each item sent this way is ready to use as a variable in PHP scripts. The script that reads in the URL automatically creates variables and assigns them values from the name/value pairs in the URL.

For example, if you had a URL for a script called *name.php3*, you could append name/value pairs after the script name to pass the script data

```
http://localhost/name.php3?name=Fred&age=45
```

You can then use the name/value pairs in the name.php3 script.

```php
<?php

print("<p>Hello $name,");

print("according to our records you are $age years old.\n");

?>
```

This script would produce the output

```
Hello Fred, according to our records you are 45 years old.
```

Additionally, you could create a link in an HTML page that passes this same information.

```html
<a href="http://localhost/name.php3?name=Fred&age=45">
Click here for name and age!</a>
```

The following scripts allow you to get input from a user and generate links containing the information that the script collects.

Script 2-4 is a form that you can use to get basic information from a user. This data includes home contact information, work contact information, and favorite hobbies, as shown in Figure 2–5.

Script 2-5 takes the data from the form and generates some links that you can use to send specific data to another script. Three links are generated. The first link is for home contact information, the second is for work contact information, and the third is for the user's favorite hobby, as shown in Figure 2–6.

Finally, Script 2-6 displays the specified data about the user, depending on which link is clicked from Script 2-5, as shown in Figure 2–7.

Script 2-4
about_you.html

```html
1. <html>
2. <head>
3. <title>Get Information to create Dynamic Links</title>
```

```
 4. </head>
 5. <body bgcolor="#FFFFFF">
 6. <h2>Please tell us a little bit about yourself</h2>
 7. <form action="generate_links.php3" method="GET">
 8. <h3>Contact Info:</h3>
 9. First Name: <input type="text" name="first_name">
10. <br>Last Name: <input type="text" name="last_name">
11. <br>Home Phone: <input type="text" name="home_phone">
12. <br>SSN: <input type="text" name="ssn">
13. <h3>Employment Info:</h3>
14. Company Name: <input type="text" name="company_name">
15. <br>Work Phone: <input type="text" name="company_phone">
16. <br>Title: <input type="text" name="title">
17. <h3>Hobbies:</h3>
18. What's your favorite hobby?
19. <br>Skiing <input type="radio" name="hobby" value="skiing">
20. <br>Rollerblading<input type="radio" name="hobby"
    value="rollerblading">
21. <br>Chess <input type="radio" name="hobby" value="chess">
22. <p><input type="submit" name="Submit" value="Submit">
23. <input type="Reset">
24. </form>
25. </body>
26. </html>
```

HOW THE SCRIPT WORKS

Script 2-4 is your basic run-of-the-mill HTML form. There are text entry fields so the user can send some information to the next script. The important part of this script is the correct naming of the text fields. You need those names in the next scripts as they will be the variable names of the data collected from the form.

Script 2-5
generate_links.php3

```
1. <html>
2. <head>
3. <title>Generated Links</title>
4. </head>
5. <body  bgcolor="#FFFFFF">
6. <h2>Links Generated Based on User Input</h2>
7. <?php
8. print("<p><a
   href=\"user.php3?first_name=$first_name&last_name=$last
   _name&home_phone=$home_phone&ssn=$ssn\">");
9. print("Contact Info</a>");
```

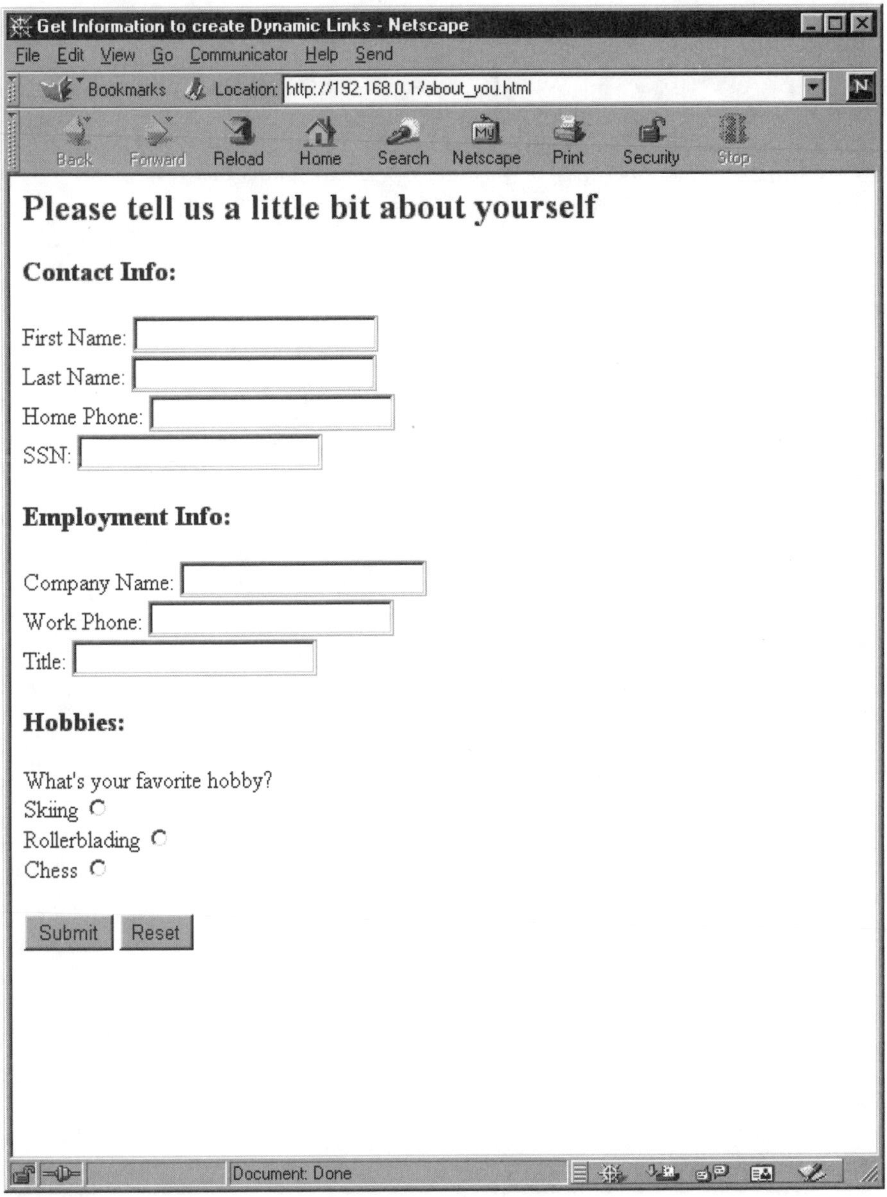

FIGURE 2–5 Output from about_you. html

FIGURE 2–6 Output from generate_links.php3

```
10. print("<p><a href=\"user.php3?company_name=$company_name&
    company_phone=$company_phone&title=$title&ssn=$ssn\">");
11. print("Work Info</a>");
12. print("<p><a href=\"user.php3?hobby=$hobby&ssn=$ssn\">");
13. print("Favorite Hobby</a>");
14. ?>
15. </body>
16. </html>
```

HOW THE SCRIPT WORKS

- Lines 1 through 6 are normal HTML.
- Line 7 is the opening PHP tag. It tells the Web server to start processing the script as PHP, and not as HTML.
- Lines 8 and 9 generate a link that passes the user's personal information to the next script.
- Lines 10 and 11 generate a link that passes the user's work information to the next script.
- Lines 12 and 13 generate a link that passes the user's favorite hobby to the next script.
- Line 14 is the close PHP tag. It tells the Web server to stop processing PHP and resume processing the page as normal HTML.
- Lines 15 and 16 close out the HTML for the page.

Script 2-6
user.php3

```
1.  <html>
2.  <head>
3.  <title>User Data from Generated Links</title>
4.  </head>
5.  <body>
6.  <ul>
7.  <li>First Name: <b><? print $first_name ?></b>
8.  <li>Last Name: <b><? print $last_name ?></b>
9.  <li>Home Phone: <b><? print $home_phone ?></b>
10. <li>SSN: <b><? print $ssn ?></b>
11. <li>Company Name: <b><? print $company_name ?></b>
12. <li>Work Phone: <b><? print $company_phone ?></b>
13. <li>Title: <b><? print $title ?></b>
14. <li>Favorite Hobby: <b><? print $hobby ?></b>
15. </ul>
16. </body>
17. </html>
```

HOW THE SCRIPT WORKS

- Lines 1 through 6 are normal HTML.
- Lines 7 through 14 print out information passed to the script from the links in Script 2-4. Not all of the information is printed out; only the information passed from the individual links is printed out.
- Lines 15 through 17 close out the HTML for the page.

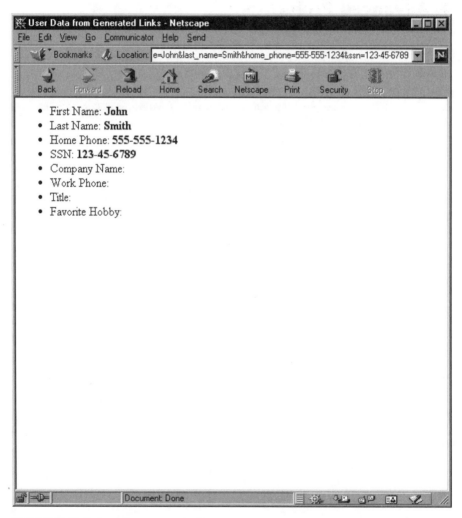

FIGURE 2-7 Output from user.php3

◆ Recap

This chapter taught you some of the basics of PHP. Of the many wonderful tools available in PHP, variables and the `print( )` function are the tools you will probably use most often. Hopefully, this chapter has helped you to get familiar with the use of variables and the basic conventions used in PHP programming.

◆ Advanced Project

Add more types of contact information to Script 2-3 and group the new information into categories, such as work experience, education, and so forth. Then modify Script 2-4 so that the generated links go to different pages, not only to Script 2-5. (Hint: read about `if/then` statements in the next chapter.) Have each of the pages contain the information for one category. In Chapter 4, "Files, Strings, and Mail," you'll learn to save this information to a file.

3 User Interaction: PHP with Forms and Cookies

IN THIS CHAPTER

- New Functions
- Creating Your Own Functions
- Checking User-Entered Data for Required Fields
- Having Fun with Cookies
- Working with Arrays

◆ User Interaction

User interaction is what the Web is all about. The more you can do to facilitate interaction, the more dynamic your site can become. Forms provide the most basic form of interaction with a user, but dynamic pages that change, or provide a more personal touch based on user's input, provide a more robust surfing experience for the user. This chapter provides more ways to interact with your users via forms, and also introduces cookies.

◆ New Functions

if/then

```
if( expression ):

        statement ;
endif;
```

31

The if/then statement is another core construct in programming. Since you are creating dynamic pages, you'll have to do different things based on different data. If the data from a form is incorrectly or improperly formatted, then you need to alert the user and have them correct the mistake.

The if/then statement allows you to test data and then take the appropriate action according to the result of the test. A simple if/then statement example is

```
if($age > '30'):
    print("You were probably born before 1970");
endif;
```

You can add an else to the statement to test for further conditions.

```
if($age > '30'):
    print("You were probably born before 1970");
else:
    print("You were probably born after 1970");
endif;
```

And further still, you can add the an elseif to the statement.

```
if($age > '30'):
    print("You were probably born before 1970");
elseif($age < '2'):
    print("You're a little young to be surfing.");
else:
    print("You were probably born after 1970");
endif;
```

There are many operators you can use in your if/then statements to evaluate data. Table 3.1 lists the most common operators you can use in your expressions to test data.

More information on if/then statements can be found in the PHP manual at *http://www.php.net/manual/html/control-structures.html*.

isset()

```
isset( variable );
```

The isset() function is a useful complement to the if/then statement to determine if a variable has been set. A perfect example of this is when the user enters information into a form. You could write a simple if/then statement to check if a user has pressed the Submit button. If the $submit variable has been set, then you can do some processing on the data that was entered from the

TABLE 3.1 Common Operators

Operator	Definition and Usage
==	The **equal** operator. Used to test if two values are the same. `if($a == $b):`
!=	The **NOT equal** operator. Used to test if two values are different. `if($a != $b):`
>	The **greater than** operator. Used to test if the first value is greater than the second value. `if($a > $b):`
<	The **less than** operator. Used to test if the first value is less than the second value. `if($a < $b):`
>=	The **greater than or equal to** operator. Used to test if the first value is greater than or equal to the second value. `if($a >= $b):`
<=	The **less than or equal to** operator. Used to test if one value is less than or equal to the second value. `if($a <= $b):`
&&	The **and** operator. Used to evaluate multiple conditions where you want all the conditions to be true. `if(($a == $b) && ($c == $d)):`
||	The **or** operator. Used to evaluate multiple conditions where you want any one of the conditions to be true. `if(($a == $b) \|\| ($c == $d)):`
!	The **NOT** operator. Used to test if a condition is false. `if(($a == $b) && !($c == $d)):`

form. If the `$submit` variable has not been set, then you know that the user hasn't entered any information into the form, and you can print the form to the browser so the user can enter data.

```
if(isset($submit)):
    //do something
else:
    //print out the form
endif;
```

You can also use the NOT operator (!) with the `isset()` function to see if a particular item in a form has been left blank. For example,

```
if(!isset($phone_number)):
        print("You didn't enter your phone number!\n");
endif;
```

More information on the `isset()` function can be found in the PHP manual at *http://www.php.net/manual/html/function.isset.html*.

date()

```
date( format );
```

The `date()` function returns just what you'd expect, the current date. The `date()` function can be used to return just about any format of date or time that you want. You need to include the date formats that you wish to use and enclose everything in quotes. Other characters, such as commas or dashes, can also be included.

```
$today = date("M j, Y");

//$today = "Jan 1, 2000" (if today was Jan 1...)
```

Table 3.2 shows the various forms you can use to format the date.

The following examples use the `date()` function with the above codes (assume the date is January 1, 2000 at 12pm).

```
$today = date("F jS, Y");
//$today = "January 1st, 2000"

$today = date("D F d, h:ia");
//$today = "Sat January 01, 12:00pm"

$today = date("l F jS");
//$today = "Saturday January 1st"
```

More information on the `date()` function can be found in the PHP manual at *http://www.php.net/manual/html/function.date.html*

time()

```
time();
```

The `time()` function probably doesn't return what you'd expect. The `time()` function returns a UNIX timestamp, which is the current number of seconds since January 1, 1970 00:00:00. The `time()` function is useful when determining the expiration date for a cookie, which is explained below.

To use the `time()` function just set a variable to it.

```
$timestamp = time();
```

More information on the `time()` function can be found in the PHP manual at *http://www.php.net/manual/html/ref.datetime.html*.

TABLE 3.2 Date Codes Used with the date() Function

Date Formats	Definitions
a	Prints out *am* or *pm* (lowercase).
A	Prints out *AM* or *PM* (uppercase).
d	Prints the numerical day of the month with leading zeros (01, 02, 03, etc.).
D	Prints the day of the week as a three letter abbreviation (Mon, Tue, Wed, etc.).
F	Prints the name of the month (January, February, etc.).
h	Prints the hour in 12-hour format.
H	Prints the hour in 24-hour format.
i	Prints the minutes (00–59).
j	Prints the day of the month with no leading zeros (1, 2, 3, etc.).
l	Prints the day of the week (Monday, Tuesday, Wednesday, etc.).
m	Prints the number of the month from 1 to 12.
M	Prints out the abbreviated name of the month (Jan, Feb, Mar, etc.).
S	Prints out the suffix for the day of the month (st, nd, rd, etc. as in 1st, 2nd, 3rd).
U	Prints the number of seconds since January 1, 1970 00:00:00 (the UNIX epoch).
y	Prints the year as two digits (98, 99, 00, etc.).
Y	Prints the year as four digits (1998, 1999, 2000, etc.).
z	Prints out the day of the year (235, 322, 365, etc.).

setcookie()

```
setcookie( name, value, expiration );
```

The `setcookie()` function allows you to set a cookie on a user's browser. A cookie is a small file that can contain any information you want. Cookies can be used to store information like usernames and other data.

The `setcookie()` function comes in two basic flavors:

- Session cookies
- Cookies that expire after a certain amount of time

Session Cookies

Session cookies are stored on the user's browser until the browser is closed. Once the browser is closed, the cookie is erased.

To create a session cookie, you simply call the `setcookie()` function in your script and provide it with a variable name and a value.

```
setcookie("username", "chris");
//equivalent to $username = chris
```

After the cookie is set, you can use the variable from the cookie on any page in your site. The variable is available up until the user closes the browser.

Cookies That Expire after X Seconds

A cookie that expires after a certain amount of time is coded like a session cookie except that you must include an expiration date. However, the way you create the expiration date is a little odd. You need to create the expiration date in seconds, but not only that, it has to be in seconds since January 1, 1970.[1] This is where the `time()` function comes in.

The `time()` function returns the number of seconds since January 1, 1970. If you want to create a cookie that expires in 30 days, you need to do the following:

1. Get the number of seconds since January 1, 1970.
2. Determine the number of seconds you want the cookie to last.
3. Add the number of seconds since January 1, 1970 to the number of seconds you want the cookie to last.

Remember that there are 86,400 seconds in a day (60 seconds * 60 minutes * 24 hours). So to create a cookie that expires in 30 days, you could do this:

```
setcookie("username", "chris", time() + (86400 * 30));
```

This function places a cookie on the user's browser for 30 days. At any time during that 30 days, you can access the variable `$username` from within the script, and it will return (in the above example) "chris."[2]

---

1. I have no clue as to why they chose that one particular date.
2. Provided, of course, the user lets you put cookies on their machine and they don't delete them during the 30-day period. Most browsers, by default, allow cookies.

To delete a cookie, simply set another cookie with the same name and no value. The following example would delete the cookie you just created.

```
setcookie("username");
```

It's also important to note that you need to set your cookies before you send any text to the browser. If you attempt to set the cookie after you send text to the browser, an error appears, warning that the cookie was not set.

More information on the `setcookie()` function can be found in the PHP manual at *http://www.php.net/manual/html/function.setcookie.html.*

Arrays

An array is a type of variable that lets you store multiple values. Let's say you have a dresser in your bedroom and it contains four drawers. In the top drawer, you have underwear; in the second drawer, you have pants; in the third drawer, you have shirts; and in the bottom drawer, you have pajamas. Being the savvy programmer that you are, you only buy designer clothes, so each item in each drawer is of a specific brand. And for simplicity, let's just assume each drawer can hold only one item (although you can have arrays with "drawers" that hold many items, or even "drawers" that hold other "dressers").

You can create an array by using the `array()` function.

```
array( name => value, name => value, …);
```

The following example shows you how to create the array and fill it with items:

```
$dresser = array(
        "underwear" => "Calvin Klein Skivvies",
        "pants" => "Ralph Lauren Pants",
        "shirts" => "Polo Shirt",
        "pajamas" => "Sears PJs"
        );
```

This creates an array with four positions. Each of the positions in the array has a generic key name, such as *shirts*. In each of these positions is an item, such as *Polo Shirt*.

To get the value of a particular item from an array, you need to specify the name of the array and the name of the position for which you want the value. To get the content of the underwear drawer in the dresser array, you would do this:

```
$item = $dresser["underwear"];
//$item = Calvin Klein Skivvies
```

You can also have an array in which you don't have name/value pairs, but only values. The construct for this type of array is slightly different.

```
array( value1, value2, value3, …);
```

Here's how to re-create the bedroom dresser array using the value-only type of array:

```
$dresser2 = array(
         "Calvin Klein Skivvies",
         "Ralph Lauren Pants",
         "Polo Shirt",
         "Sears PJs"
         );
```

In the example above, you would probably assume that the Calvin Klein Skivvies are in the first position of the array. While they are technically in the first position, PHP indexes the first position of an array as zero. The second position is indexed as one, and so on.

To get a particular item out of this array, you need to specify the name of the array and the index (position) of the item for which you want the value. To get the value of the item in position 1 of the *dresser2* array, you would do this (remember that array indexes start at zero, not one):

```
$item = $dresser2[1];
//$item = Ralph Lauren Pants
```

It's up to you how you want to set up your arrays. If you were creating an address book utility and storing information in an array, then it may be easier to use the first method where each item in the array is indexed by a name, or key, as it is also called. If you were creating a list of to-do items, then the second method may suit your needs better.

More information about arrays can be found in the PHP manual at *http://www.php.net/manual/html/language.types.array.html*.

◆ Creating Your Own Functions

Now that you are armed with the basic building blocks—variables, the print() function, and the if/then statement—you can build your own functions for use in your scripts. Creating a function is easy. You need to give your function a name, list any arguments that you will pass to the function, and list the statements that make up your function. Arguments to a function are usually data that you want the function to process in one way or another. You must also enclose the statements in your function with curly braces.

```
function name ( arg1, arg2, arg3, ...) {
    statements;
    }
```

You can define as many or as few arguments to pass to your function as you'd like. You can even choose not to define any arguments.

The most basic example of a function declaration is

```
1. function name_print($name) {
2. print("<p>Name: <b>$name</b>");
3. }
```

This function takes one argument, the variable $name, then prints some information, including the argument, to the browser.

When you want to call this function from within your script, you need to provide the function name and the exact number of arguments that you specified when you created your function. In the example above, there is only one argument specified. You can use the above function in your script like this:

```
name_print("Johnny");
```

You could also pass a variable to the function.

```
$first_name = "Johnny";
name_print($first_name);
```

The real benefit of a user-defined function is that it can save you time in coding your scripts. For instance, you could use the above example every time you needed to print a name. Instead of typing `print("<p>Name: <b>$name</b>");` every time you needed to print a name out, you could just use `name_print($name);`. Although this example doesn't really show much of a time savings, the upcoming form-checking script will show you just how much time you can save, and how much cleaner your scripts can be using functions for repetitive tasks in your scripts.

More information on functions can be found in the PHP manual at *http://www.php.net/manual/html/functions.html.*

◆ Checking User-Entered Data for Required Fields

If there's one thing you can trust a user to do, it's to NOT enter the required information into a form. You can use bold red text or big red stars, noting that certain fields are required, but time after time, if you don't have some mechanism to check for complete and correct information from the form, you'll get incomplete and often useless data.

Script 3-1 is a multipurpose script. It asks users for some basic contact information and then checks to see that the required fields have been entered. Finally, it brings the user to a confirmation screen so they can double-check to make certain all of their information is correct, as seen in Figures 3–1, 3–2, and 3–3.

The script uses three *user-defined* functions to accomplish the task at hand. The first function is the print_form function, which just prints out the form. If any of the fields have been previously entered, the function automatically enters the values into the fields. This is a nice feature so users don't have to constantly reenter all of their information just because they previously failed to enter information into one of the required fields.

The next function is the check_form function, which checks the user-entered data for the required fields. If one of the required fields has not been entered, the function tells the user what fields have not been entered and then calls the print_form function to redisplay the form so that the user can enter in the required fields.

The final function is the confirm_form function, which just displays the information that the user entered. In a real-world scenario, you could have a Confirm button on the page to let the user make sure everything is correct before sending the information to the server for whatever processing you need to do with the data.

Script 3-1
form_checker.php3

```
1.  <html>
2.  <head>
3.  <title>Contact Info Checker</title>
4.  </head>
5.  <body bgcolor="#FFFFFF">
6.  <?php
```

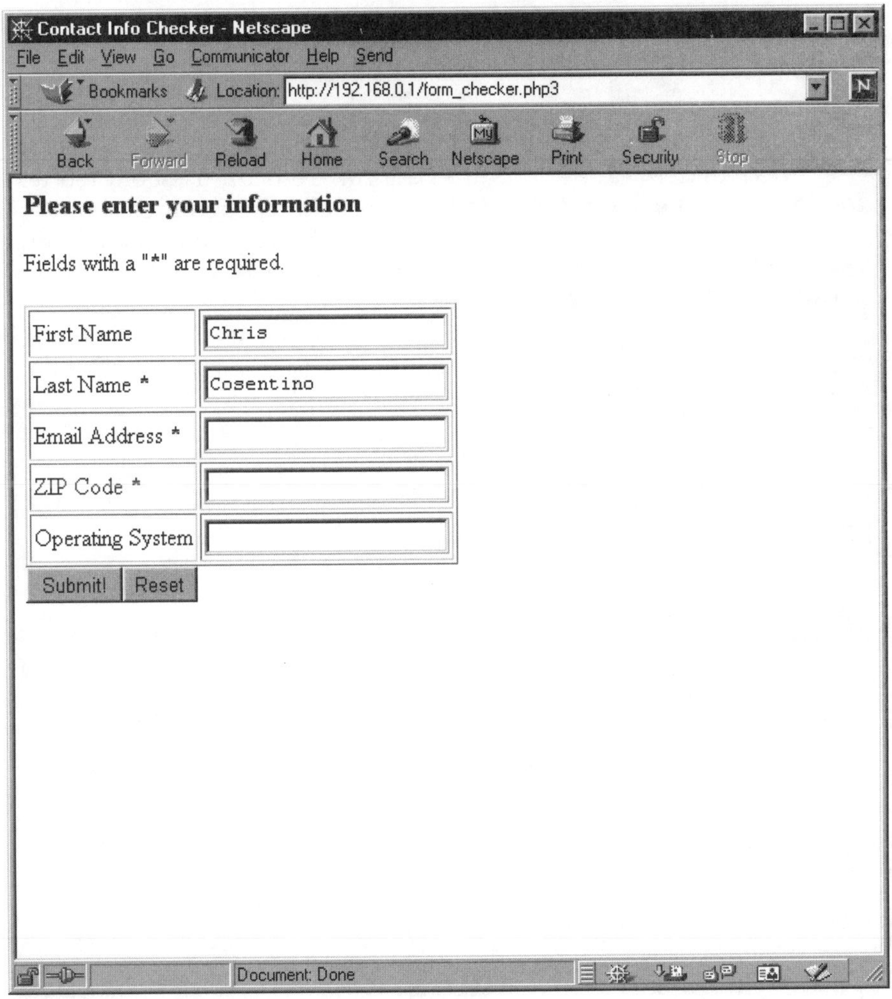

FIGURE 3–1 Output from form_checker.php3

```
 7. /* Declare some functions */
 8. function print_form($f_name, $l_name, $email, $zip, $os) {
 9. ?>
10. <form action="form_checker.php3" method="post">
11. <table cellspacing="2" cellpadding="2" border="1">
12. <tr>
13. <td>First Name</td><td><input type="text" name="f_name"
14. value="<?php print $f_name ?>"></td>
15. </tr>
16. <tr>
```

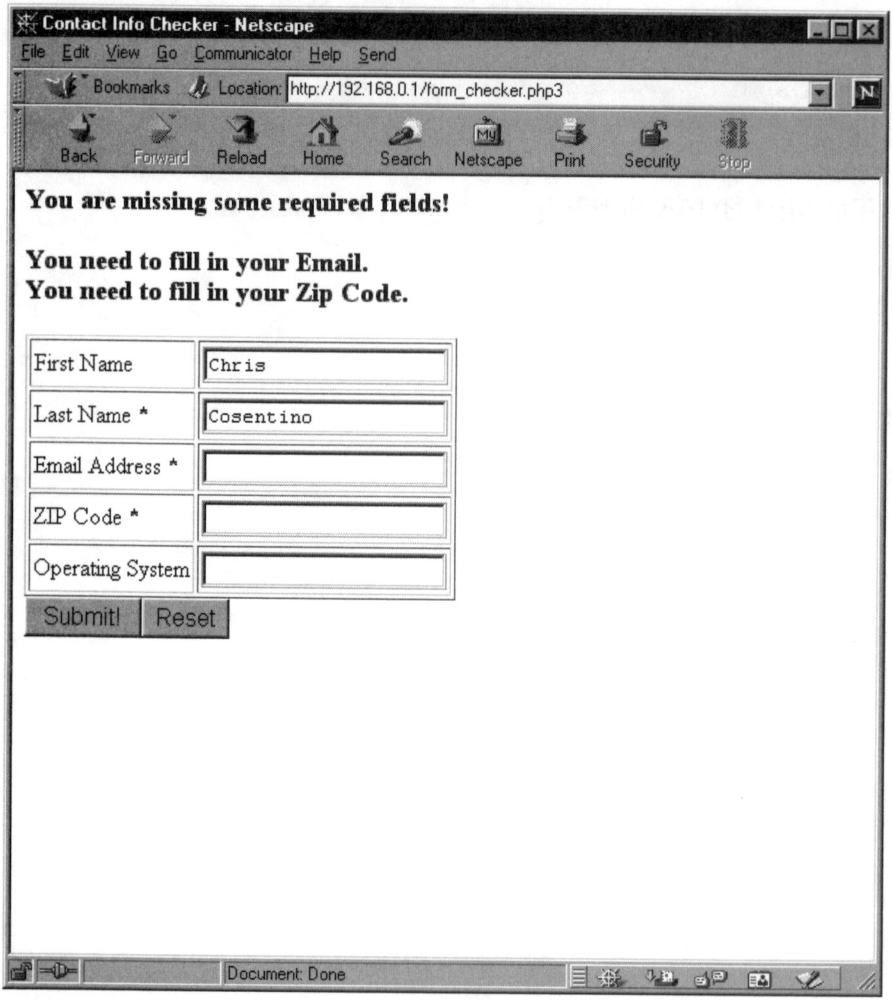

FIGURE 3-2 Output from form_checker.php3 when errors were submitted

```
17. <td>Last Name <b>*</b></td><td><input type="text"
    name="l_name"
18. value="<?php print $l_name ?>"></td>
19. </tr>
20. <tr>
21. <td>Email Address <b>*</b></td><td><input type="text"
    name="email"
22. value="<?php print $email ?>"></td>
23. </tr>
24. <tr>
```

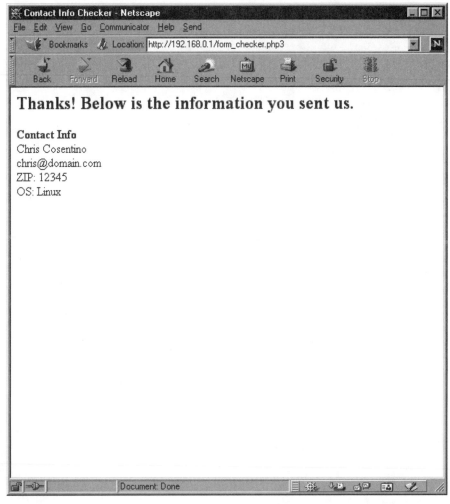

FIGURE 3–3 Output from form_checker.php3 when correct information was submitted

```
25. <td>ZIP Code <b>*</b></td><td><input type="text" name="zip"
26. value="<?php print $zip ?>"></td>
27. </tr>
28. <tr>
29. <td>Operating System</td><td><input type="text" name="os"
30. value="<?php print $os ?>"></td>
31. </tr>
32. </table>
33. <input type="submit" name="submit" value="Submit!"><input
    type="Reset">
```

```
34. </form>
35. <?
36. }
37. function check_form($f_name, $l_name, $email, $zip, $os) {
38. if(!$l_name || !$email || !$zip):
39. print("<h3>You are missing some required fields!<h3>");
40. if(!$l_name) {
41. print("You need to fill in your <b>Last Name</b>.<br>"); }
42. if(!$email) {
43. print("You need to fill in your <b>Email</b>.<br>"); }
44. if(!$zip){
45. print("You need to fill in your <b>Zip Code</b>.<br>"); }
46. print_form($f_name, $l_name, $email, $zip, $os);
47. else:
48. confirm_form($f_name, $l_name, $email, $zip, $os);
49. endif;
50. }
51. function confirm_form($f_name, $l_name, $email, $zip, $os) {
52. ?>
53. <h2>Thanks! Below is the information you sent us.</h2>
54. <b>Contact Info</b>
55. <?
56. print("<br>$f_name $l_name<br>$email<br>ZIP: $zip<br>OS:
    $os\n");
57. }
58. /* Begin Main Program */
59. if(!$submit):
60. ?>
61. <h3>Please enter your information</h3>
62. Fields with a "<b>*</b>" are required.<p>
63. <?php
64. print_form("","","","","","");
65. else:
66. check_form($f_name, $l_name, $email, $zip, $os);
67. endif;
68. ?>
69. </body>
70. </html>
```

HOW THE SCRIPT WORKS

- Lines 1 through 5 are normal HTML.
- Line 6 is the PHP start tag. It tells the Web server to start evaluating the page as PHP rather than as HTML
- Line 7 is a comment giving information to other programmers who may work on the script.
- Line 8 is the function declaration for the `print_form` function. Listed as arguments are the `$f_name`, `$l_name`, `$email`,

$zip, and $os variables. These variables all get passed to the script so that they can be automatically filled in if the user neglects to enter in some of the required information. If it's the first load of the script, then all the variables have blank (null) values.

- Line 9 is the PHP end tag. Here the script pops out of PHP and back into HTML for a few lines
- Lines 10 through 13 are normal HTML that is setting up the table and form.
- Line 14 is a continuation of the input tag in the previous line, but note the value of the input field. The script is printing the values of the variable $f_name in the field, using PHP. Notice the start and end PHP tags in this line. If the user filled in this field previously, but neglected to fill in one of the required fields, then the script automatically reinserts the user's previous information when the form is reprinted. Of course, the first time that the script is used, all the values of the variables are empty, so nothing is entered in for the values.
- Lines 18, 22, 26, and 30 serve the same function as line 14, only with different variables.
- Line 35 is a PHP start tag. This is required here at the end of the function so you can include the close curly brace, }. This tells the server that everything from the beginning of the function to this close curly brace is part of the function and should only be displayed if the function is called later in the script, regardless if the text is in PHP or plain HTML.
- Line 36 is the close curly brace that ends the function.
- Line 37 is the function declaration for the check_form function. Listed as arguments are the $f_name, $1_name, $email, $zip, and $os variables. These are the same variables that are listed in the print_form function. Since the check_form function complements the print_form function, the script uses those same variables.
- Line 38 checks to see if the user has entered the required fields. It could be read literally as: *If the last name is empty or email is empty or zip is empty, then…*
- Line 39 is executed if any of the conditions in the previous line are true. It simply prints out the text telling the user that some of the required fields have not been entered.
- Lines 40, 42, and 44 are all similar, but they are checking for different required fields. These lines are only executed if any of the conditions in line 38 are true. Each of the lines

checks to see if their value has been entered. If their value has not been entered, then they execute their subsequent line that notifies the user that the required field was not filled in.

- Lines 41, 43, and 45 are the lines that are executed if the condition in the previous lines is true.
- Line 46 is executed only if any of the conditions in line 38 are true. It recalls the `print_form` function, only this time any of the values that have been previously entered into the form will be automatically filled in by the script as the form is printed to the browser.
- Line 47 is used when none of the conditions in line 38 are met—if all of the required fields have been entered into the form.
- Line 48 calls the `confirm_form` function to print out the information that has been submitted to the server.
- Line 49 completes the `if/then/else` statement.
- Line 50 is the close curly brace that ends the `check_form` function.
- Line 51 is the function declaration for the `confirm_form` function. Listed as arguments are the `$f_name`, `$l_name`, `$email`, `$zip`, and `$os` variables. These are the same variables that are listed in both the `print_form` and `check-form` functions. Since the `confirm_form` function complements the `print_form` function, the script uses the same variables.
- Line 52 is the end PHP tag. After this line, the Web server reads the page as normal HTML for a few more lines.
- Lines 53 through 56 simply print out the information that the user has entered.
- Line 57 is the close curly brace that ends the `confirm_form` function.
- Line 58 is a comment that informs other programmers working on the script that the "main" part of the script begins here.
- Lines 59 through 67 execute the script. Literally, it could be read as: *If the Submit button has NOT been pushed, then print out a blank form. Else, if the Submit button has been pushed, check the form to see if the required fields were entered.*
- Line 59 checks to see if the Submit button was pushed.
- If the Submit button has not been pushed, then lines 60 through 62 escape from PHP for a moment and print some instructions to the browser.

- At lines 63 and 64, the script returns to PHP and calls the `print_form` function, sending blanks ("") to initialize all the variables.
- If the Submit button has been pushed, then lines 65 and 66 are executed and the `check_form` function is called to check the data.
- Line 67 ends the `if/then/else` statement started in line 59.
- Lines 68 through 70 escape from PHP once again and print out the closing HTML to the browser.

◆ Having Fun with Cookies

Once you get a user to provide you with some information, you can provide them a more customized experience. Cookies allow you to store information, such as a person's name and email address, on that person's Web browser. When a user subsequently visits the site, you can use information from the cookie in your script.

Setting a cookie is simple. You only need to enter the name of the variable you want to store and its value. The following example sets a cookie on the user's browser with the variable name `f_name` and a value of *Chris:*

```
setcookie("Chris", $f_name);
```

Script 3-2 is a simple script that asks a user for their first name and then stores the first name, along with the date, to a cookie on the user's browser, as shown in Figure 3–4. The cookie will remain there for one year (`time() + (365 * 86400)`). Subsequent visits to the site greet the user with a customized message telling them the last time they accessed the site, as shown in Figure 3–5.

Script 3-2
cookie.php3

```
1.  <?php
2.  if(isset($f_name)):
3.  /* reset the cookie if there was a cookie previously */
4.  setcookie("f_name",$f_name, time() + 365 * 86400);
5.   /* set the old date to the date from the cookie */
6.  if(isset($date)):
7.  $old_date = $date;
8.  else:
```

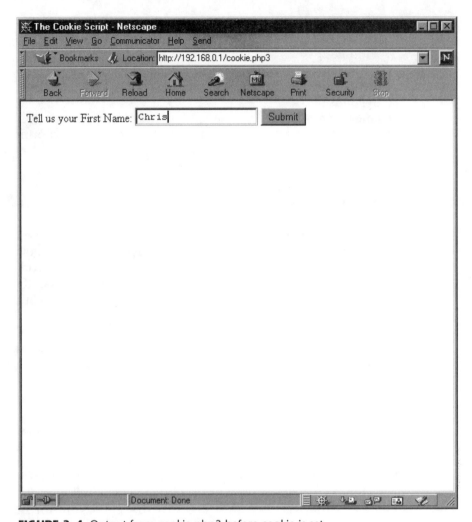

FIGURE 3–4 Output from cookie.php3 before cookie is set

```
 9. $old_date = date("l F j, Y");
10. endif;
11. $date = date("l F j, Y");
12. /* reset the date in the cookie to today */
13. setcookie("date", $date, time() + 365 * 86400);
14. endif;
15. ?>
16. <html>
17. <head>
18. <title>The Cookie Script</title>
```

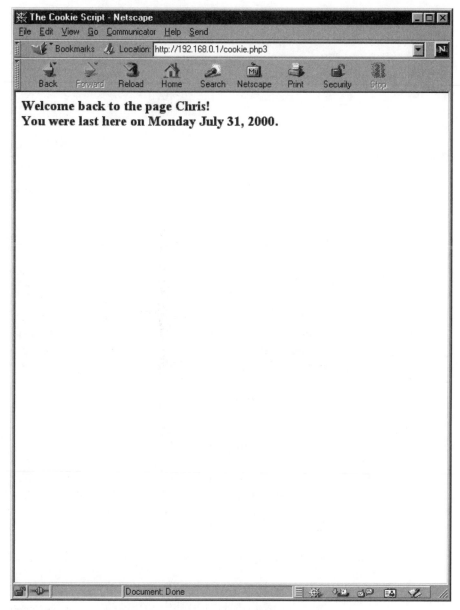

FIGURE 3–5 Output from cookie.php3 after cookie is set

```
19.  </head>
20.  <body>
21.  <?php
22.  if(isset($f_name)):
23.  ?>
24.  <h3>Welcome back to the page <?php print $f_name ?>!
25.  <br>You were last here on <?php print $old_date ?>.</h3>
26.  <?php
27.  else:
28.  ?>
29.  <form action="cookie.php3" method="POST">
30.  Tell us your First Name: <input type="text" name="f_name">
31.  <input type="submit" name="submit" value="Submit">
32.  </form>
33.  <?
34.  endif;
35.  ?>
36.  </body>
37.  </html>
```

HOW THE SCRIPT WORKS

- Line 1 is the PHP start tag. For this script, you need to go right into PHP because you have to set any cookies before you send text to the browser.
- Line 2 checks to see if the $f_name variable is set. The $f_name variable could have been set from the form, or a preexisting cookie from a previous visit to the page may have set it. If the variable has not been set, then the script continues without doing anything.
- Line 4 sets the cookie for the $f_name variable. You use the time() function to get the current time and add that to 1 year. This allows the cookie to stay on the user's browser for one year or until the user deletes the cookie.
- If the $date variable is set (in the cookie), then lines 6 through 10 set the value of the $old_date variable to the value of the $date variable (from the cookie). This is done so that we can reference the last time the user was on the page. If the $date variable was not set in the cookie, then the $old_date variable is just set to the current date.
- Line 11 sets the $date variable to the current date.
- Line 13 sets the cookie for the $date variable. Just like the $f_name variable, you set it to expire in one year.
- Line 14 ends the if/then/else statement that started on line 2.

- Line 15 is the PHP end tag.
- Lines 17 through 20 print out the plain HTML headers for the page.
- Line 22 checks to see if the $f_name variable has been set.
- If the $f_name variable has been set, then lines 24 and 25 greet the user with a customized message telling them the day that they last accessed the page.
- If the $f_name variable has not been set, then lines 27 through 32 print out a form asking the user to enter their first name.
- Line 34 ends the if/then/else statement that started on line 22.
- Lines 35 through 37 end the PHP part of the page and print out the closing HTML tags.

◆ Working with Arrays

This next script, Script 3-3, shows an example of how to create two arrays, one indexed by keys and the other indexed by position (index). The script also illustrates how to get the values out of the arrays, as shown in Figure 3–6.

Script 3-3
array.php3

```
1.  <html>
2.  <head>
3.  <title>Arrays</title>
4.  </head>
5.  <body bgcolor="#FFFFFF">
6.  <h2>An Array of Clothes</h2>
7.  <?
8.  $dresser = array(
9.          "underwear" => "Calvin Klein Skivvies",
10.         "pants" => "Ralph Lauren Pants",
11.         "shirts" => "Polo Shirt",
12.         "pajamas" => "Sears PJs"
13.         );
14.         $keyed1 = $dresser["underwear"];
15.         $keyed2 = $dresser["pants"];
16.         $keyed3 = $dresser["shirts"];
17.         $keyed4 = $dresser["pajamas"];
18.
19.  $dresser2 = array(
```

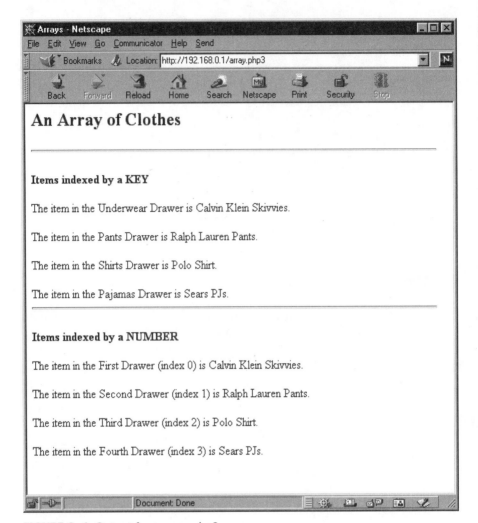

FIGURE 3–6 Output from array.php3

```
20.            "Calvin Klein Skivvies",
21.            "Ralph Lauren Pants",
22.            "Polo Shirt",
23.            "Sears PJs"
24.            );
25.            $numbered1 = $dresser2[0];
26.            $numbered2 = $dresser2[1];
27.            $numbered3 = $dresser2[2];
28.            $numbered4 = $dresser2[3];
29. ?>
30. <hr>
```

```
31. <h4>Items indexed by a KEY</h4>
32. <p>The item in the Underwear Drawer is <? print $keyed1 ?>.
33. <p>The item in the Pants Drawer is <? print $keyed2 ?>.
34. <p>The item in the Shirts Drawer is <? print $keyed3 ?>.
35. <p>The item in the Pajamas Drawer is <? print $keyed4 ?>.
36. <hr>
37. <h4>Items indexed by a NUMBER</h4>
38. <p>The item in the First Drawer (index 0) is <? print
    $numbered1 ?>.
39. <p>The item in the Second Drawer (index 1) is <? print
    $numbered2 ?>.
40. <p>The item in the Third Drawer (index 2) is <? print
    $numbered3 ?>.
41. <p>The item in the Fourth Drawer (index 3) is <? print
    $numbered4 ?>.
42. </body>
43. </html>
```

HOW THE SCRIPT WORKS

- Lines 1 through 6 are normal HTML.
- Line 7 is the PHP start tag.
- Lines 8 through 13 create the dresser1 array and fill it with keys and values.
- Lines 14 through 17 set a variable for each of the items in the array. You'll use these to print out the contents of the array later in the script.
- Lines 19 through 24 create the dresser2 array and fill it with values.
- Lines 25 through 28 set a variable for each of the items in this array. You'll use these to print out the contents of the array later in the script.
- Line 29 is the close PHP tag.
- Lines 32 through 35 print out the variables that you created in lines 14 through 17.
- Lines 38 through 41 print out the variables that you created in lines 19 through 24.
- Lines 42 and 43 close out the HTML for the page.

◆ Recap

This chapter introduced some more of the building blocks of PHP.

- if/then Statements
- Custom functions
- Cookies

if/then statements are by far one of the most often used constructs in PHP (and maybe programming in general). Take the time to understand how the various operators work in if/then statements; it's time well spent. Also practice writing your own functions for parts of your script that seem to repeat. If you have chunks of code that are the same throughout the script, there is probably a good possibility that the particular chunk of code could be created as a function and reused throughout the script. Finally, make sure you are familiar with cookies. You'll find them invaluable for storing user-specific data that can be used in many of your scripts.

◆ Advanced Project

Modify Script 3-3 so that it asks for more of the user's information. For example, ask them for their birthday, then have the script check the birthday variable on the user's browser and compare it to the current date. If the two dates are the same (if it's their birthday), then present the user with a special birthday greeting.

4 Files, Strings, and Mail

IN THIS CHAPTER

- New Functions
- Opening and Displaying the Contents of a File
- Using String Functions to Check Data
- Creating a Simple Feedback Script
- Project: Customer Service Feedback Page

◆ More Tools for Your PHP Arsenal

This chapter introduces you to the file and string functions in PHP. You'll learn how to open and access files, manipulate strings, and write data to a file. You'll also learn about the quick and easy `mail()` function, which lets you easily send email from any script.[1] These scripts build heavily from material in Chapter 2, "Your First Dynamic Web Pages," and Chapter 3, "User Interaction: PHP With Forms and Cookies," so be sure you've read over that material and played around with a few of the example scripts.

---

1. No more of those awkward and cryptic CGI scripts to configure for simple emails!

◆ New Functions

fopen() and fclose()

```
fopen( filename, mode );
fclose( filename );
```

The `fopen()` and `fclose()` functions are used in PHP to open and close files. `fopen()` is especially useful because it provides the ability to open files via the HTTP or FTP protocol in addition to the ability to open files that are on your local server. To open a file, you simply need to specify the name of the file (including the path to the file, if necessary) and the mode you want to open it in. Table 4.1 details the various modes you can use when opening files. The example below opens the file *myfile.txt* in read mode, denoted by the *r*. The open file is assigned to the variable `$file`. Once the file is opened, you can begin processing the data in the file by referring to the variable that you assigned.[2]

TABLE 4.1 Options for Opening Files

Mode	Definition and Usage
a	Open the file for appending (adding) data. The data will be added to the end of the file. `fopen("myfile.txt", "a");`
a+	Open the file for reading and appending data. The data will be added to the end of the file. `fopen("myfile.txt", "a+");`
r	Open the file for reading only (this option must be specified if using HTTP to open the file). `fopen("myfile.txt", "r");`
r+	Open the file for reading and writing. The data will be added to the beginning of the file. `fopen("myfile.txt", "r+");`
w	Open the file for writing only. If the file exists, all data is deleted and replaced by the new data you add. If the file doesn't exist, PHP will try to create it. `fopen("myfile.txt", "w");`
w+	Open the file for reading and writing. If the file exists, all data will be lost and replaced by the new data you add. If the file doesn't exist, PHP will try to create it. `fopen("myfile.txt", "w+");`

---

2. This is also referred to as a *file handle*.

```
$file = fopen("myfile.txt", "r");
```

When attempting to open or create files, be sure that the permissions are set correctly in the directory so PHP can access the file.

When you are done with the file, you must close it with the `fclose()` function. You must specify the variable that you assigned to the file when it was opened.

```
fclose($file);
```

File Processing Functions

After you open a file, there are several functions to get information in or out of the file. Table 4.2 lists some of the more common functions used for reading from and writing to files.

For the complete list of file functions, refer to the PHP manual at *http://www.php.net/manual/ref.filesystem.php3.*

String Functions

Once you pull some data out of a file, you may want to find out information about that data or to clean it up by taking out white space or new line characters. There are several functions that let

TABLE 4.2 Functions for Accessing Files

Function	Definition and Usage
fpassthru()	Reads the entire content of the file and prints the output to the browser. Note: you do not need to use `fclose()` to close the file if you use this function. This function automatically closes the file. `fpassthru($file);`

fgets()	Reads in a string for a file up to a certain amount of characters minus one.[a] If the end of the file is reached in the file before the specified amount of characters is reached, `fgets()` simply returns the entire file.
	`fgets($file, 101);`
	`//Reads in the first 100 characters of the file.`

fgetss()	The exact same as `fgets()`, only this function strips out any PHP or HTML code it encounters. `fgetss($file, 65);`
fputs() fwrite()	These two functions both write data to the specified file. Be sure to put in newline characters when appropriate.[b] `fputs($file, "I'm adding a line to the file.\n");`

[a] I have no clue why it is implemented like this, but if you want the first 100 characters of a file, you need to put 101 after the filename in this function.

[b] This is one function with two names. Use whichever suits you; they are exactly the same. Another PHP oddity.

you do these tasks and more. Table 4.3 lists some of the more common string functions.

For the complete list of file functions, refer to the PHP manual at *http://www.php.net/manual/ref.strings.php3.*

mail()

```
mail( to, subject, body, additional_headers );
```

And now the moment you have been waiting for. This function is a simple way to send email from a script. The `mail()` function is probably one of the simplest ways to add more power to your site. If a user registers with your site or provides feedback, you can eas-

TABLE 4.3 String Functions

Function	Definition and Usage
substr()	Reads in part of a string (substring). You need to specify the string, starting point, and end point of the substring you want to return. If the starting point is a positive number, then the function counts from the left side of the string. If the starting point is a negative number, then the function counts from the right side of the string.

	Usage: substr(STRING, Starting Character, Number of Characters)
	`$nickname = substr("Patrick", 0, 3);`
	`// $nickname = "Pat"`
	`$nickname = substr("Patrick", -4, 4);`
	`// $nickname = "rick"`

strlen()	Returns the length of a string.
	`$length = strlen("Patrick");`
	`// $length = 7`

trim()	Trims white space from the left and right side of a string.
	`$trimmed = trim("      Wasted Space    ");`
	`// $trimmed = "Wasted Space"`

htmlentities()	This function encodes the data in HTML. For example, quotes are encoded as ", less-than signs are encoded as <, and so on.
	This function is useful if you want to display data to a browser that contains characters that may interfere with the browser's ability to render that data. `$fixed_data = htmlentities($data);`

	Although not really a string function, you can use the dot (.) operator to append two strings together.
	`$sentence = "This is a ";`
	`$sentence .= "complete sentence.";`
	`//$sentence = "This is a complete sentence."`

ily send them an email to thank them, and you can send the user-entered information to any number of administrators for the site.

Use of the `mail()` function is simple. You need to specify

- Who to send the mail to
- The subject of the mail
- The body of the message

You can also send additional headers, such as who the mail is from, but it is not required in the function.

```
$to = "dino@bedrock.com";
$subject = "Beware of the Goodtimes Virus!";
$body = "Ha! It's a Hoax!\n";
$from = "FROM: Fred Flintstone <fred@bedrock.com>";
mail($to, $subject, $body, $from);
```

Additional info on the `mail()` function can be found in the PHP manual at *http://www.php.net/manual/function.mail.php3*.

◆ Opening and Displaying the Contents of a File

Here is a simple script that allows you to safely display the contents of any text-based file in a browser. Often when you're reading in information from a file and displaying it to a browser, you may run into situations where the data being read in and displayed interferes with how the browser displays the information. Characters such as quotes, less-than signs, and greater-than signs can cause the data to be incorrectly displayed because the browser is trying to render everything as HTML. This script solves that problem by encoding special characters with HTML code. Script 4-1 opens itself and displays its contents to the browser, as shown in Figures 4–1 and 4–2.

Script 4-1
file_read.php3

```
1. <?php
2. $file = fopen("file_read.php3", "r");
3. $data = fread($file, 1000);
4. $fixed_data = htmlentities($data);
5. print("<pre>$fixed_data<pre>");
6. ?>
```

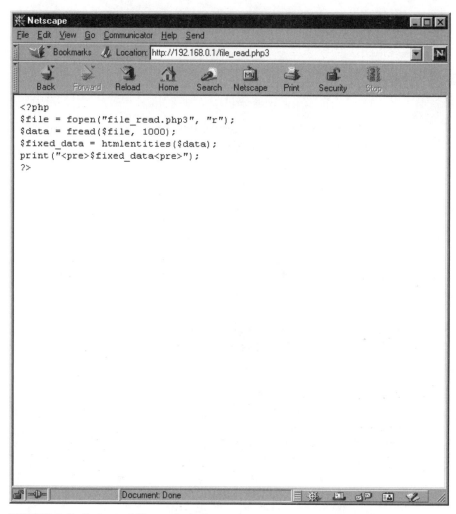

```
<?php
$file = fopen("file_read.php3", "r");
$data = fread($file, 1000);
$fixed_data = htmlentities($data);
print("<pre>$fixed_data<pre>");
?>
```

FIGURE 4-1 Output of file_read.php3

HOW THE SCRIPT WORKS

- Line 1 is the PHP start tag. It tells the Web server to start evaluating the page as PHP rather than as HTML. In the case of this script, there is no static HTML at all.
- Line 2 opens the file for reading. The script assigns the open file to the file handle $file.
- Line 3 reads in the first 1,000 characters of the file. The limit is set to 1,000 because we want to read in the entire file and

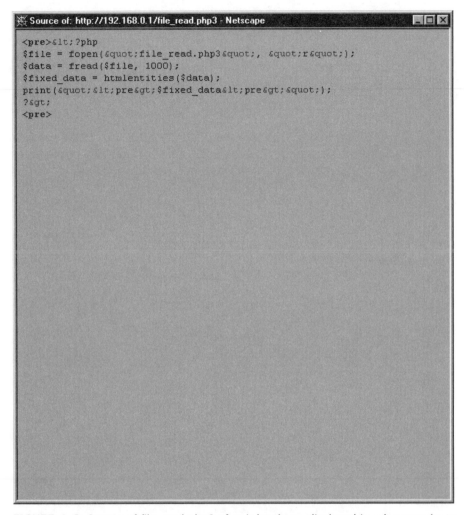

FIGURE 4–2 Source of file_read.php3 after it has been displayed in a browser (note the HTML entries)

we know that the file is less than 1,000 characters long, so the whole file is read in. The contents of the file are assigned to the variable $data.

- Line 4 encodes all the special characters read from the file as HTML code so that it can be viewed in a browser. This is done by using the htmlentities() function on $data (the contents of the file). The result of this operation is assigned to the variable $fixed_data.

- Line 5 prints out the file. The <pre> tag is used to preserve the new lines and spacing of the data.
- Line 6 is the close PHP tag (and the end of this script).

◆ Using String Functions to Check Data

The string functions in PHP give you a lot of power to disassemble and process strings and is especially useful when checking data received from a form. Script 4-2 checks a US zip code field to see if it has the correct number of characters for a zip code, as shown in Figures 4–3 and 4–4. If the data is five characters, then we can assume it is probably a valid US zip code, but what about the zip+4 zip code format? This script tests to see if the zip code is a five-digit zip or a zip+4, and if it is neither, it returns an error, as shown in Figure 4–5.

Script 4–2
zip_check.php3

```
1.  <html>
2.  <head>
3.  <title>ZIP Code Checker</title>
4.  </head>
5.  <body>
6.  <?php
7.  if(isset($submit));
8.      $zip = trim($zip);
9.      $zip_length = strlen($zip);
10.     $zip_test = substr($zip, -5, 1);
11.     if(($zip_length > '5' && $zip_test != '-') || ($zip_length <
    '5')):
12.         ?>
13.         <p>That doesn't appear to be a valid ZIP or ZIP+4
    ZIP code.
14.         <p>ZIP codes should be in the format of "12345" or "12345-
    1234".
15.         <?
16.     else:
17.             print("Thanks. Now that's a good ZIP code!");
18.     endif;
19.  else:
20.  ?>
21.  <form action="zip_check.php3" method="POST">
22.  Please enter your Zip code: <input type="text" name="zip"
    size="10" maxlength="10">
```

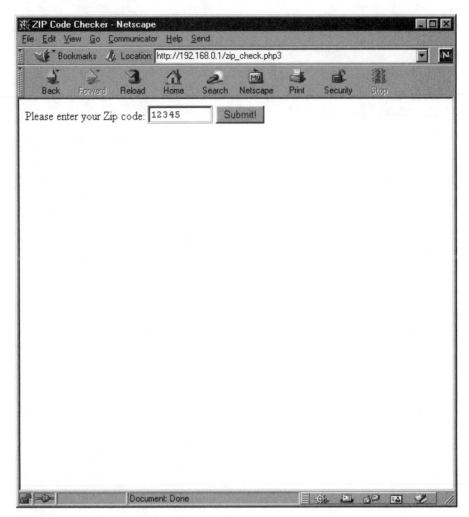

FIGURE 4-3 The zip_check.php3 script

```
23. <input type="submit" name="submit" value="Submit!">
24. </form>
25. <?
26. endif;
27. ?>
28. </body>
29. </html>
```

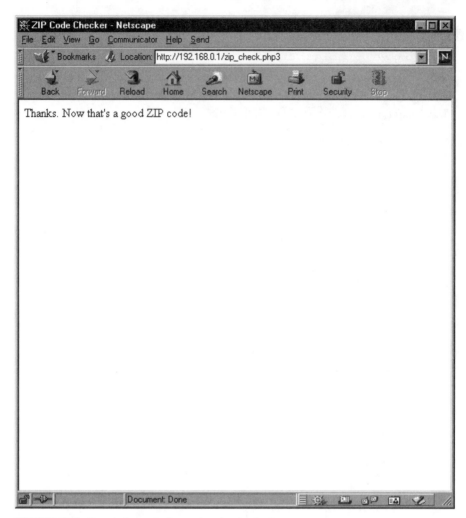

FIGURE 4–4 Good zip code from zip_check.php3

HOW THE SCRIPT WORKS

- Lines 1 through 5 are normal HTML.
- Line 6 is the PHP start tag. It tells the Web server to start evaluating the page as PHP rather than as HTML.
- Line 7 checks to see if the Submit button has been pressed. If it has, then the script continues with line 8; if it has not, the script goes to line 18.

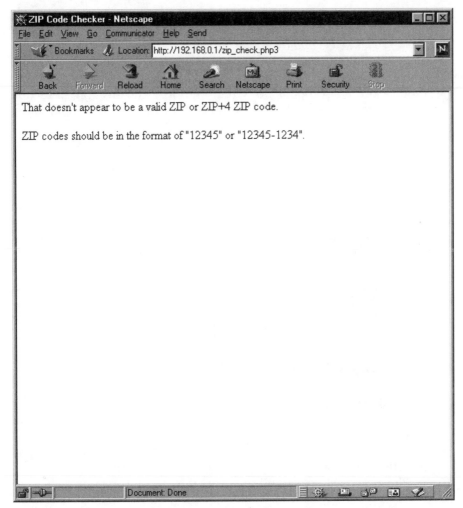

FIGURE 4–5 Bad zip code from zip_check.php3

- Line 8 trims out any white space the user may have entered before or after the zip code.
- Line 9 gets the length of the zip code and puts it into the variable $zip_length. Later in the script, the length is used to determine if the zip is correctly formatted.
- Line 10 gets the character that is 5 spaces back from the last character and puts it into the variable $zip_test. See the next line for why it does this.

- Line 11 tests to see if the zip code that the user entered is valid. It can read literally as: *If the zip code is more than 5 characters and the 6th character is not the – sign, then it is not a valid zip. Also, if the zip code is less than five characters, it is not a valid zip.*
- If the zip code is not valid, then lines 12 through 15 escape from PHP and print some text to the browser, telling the user of the invalid zip code.
- If the zip code was valid, line 17 tells the user that the zip code is acceptable.
- Line 18 ends the `if/then/else` statement that started on line 10.
- Lines 19 through 24 are executed if the Submit button was not pressed. These lines print the form to the browser so the user can enter a valid zip. Note that the form limits the number of characters that can be entered into the field to 10 characters.
- Lines 25 through 27 end the `if/then/else` statement started on line 7.
- Lines 28 and 29 close out the HTML page.

◆ Creating a Simple Feedback Script

Feedback from users is always a good way to get input on your site and to make improvements accordingly. While it is possible to set up a simple email link asking for feedback, Script 4-3 keeps the user on your site and eliminates the need to launch a separate application to send email, as seen in Figures 4–6 and 4–7. Plus it's easy to code and integrate into existing Web pages.

Script 4–3
feedback.php3

```
1.  <html>
2.  <head>
3.  <title>Feedback</title>
4.  </head>
5.  <body>
6.  <?php
7.  if(isset($submit)):
8.      $to = "webmaster@domain.com";
9.      $subject = "Feedback for the Website!";
10.     $body = "A user has entered feedback on the site!\n";
```

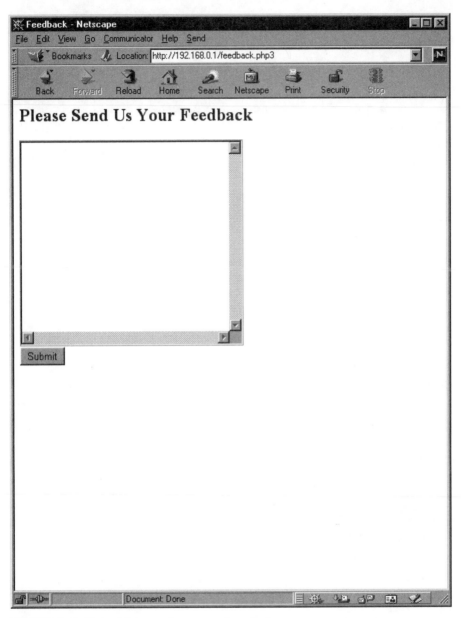

FIGURE 4–6 Output from customer_service.php3

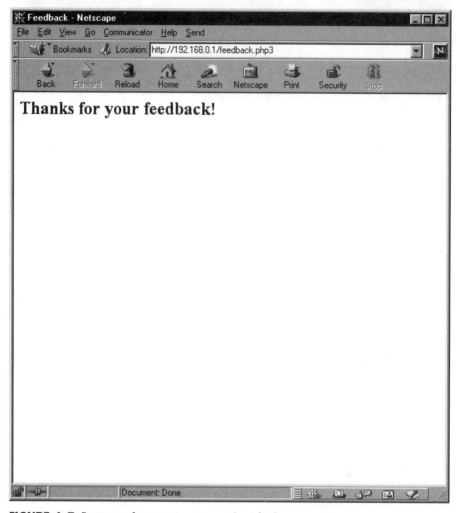

FIGURE 4–7 Response from customer_service.php3

```
11.    $body .= "Their feedback is:\n\n";
12.    $body .= $feedback;
13.    mail($to, $subject, $body);
14.    print("<h2>Thanks for your feedback!</h2>");
15. else:
16. ?>
17. <form action="feedback.php3" method="POST">
18. <h2>Please Send Us your Feedback</h2>
19. <textarea cols=35 rows=15 name="feedback">
20. </textarea>
```

```
21. <br>
22. <input type="submit" name="submit" value="Submit">
23. </form>
24. <?
25. endif;
26. ?>
27. </body>
28. </html>
```

HOW THE SCRIPT WORKS

- Lines 1 through 5 are normal HTML.
- Line 6 is the PHP start tag. It tells the Web server to start evaluating the page as PHP rather than as HTML.
- Line 7 checks to see if the Submit button has been pushed. If it has, then the script continues with line 8. If it has not, then the script continues with line 15.
- Lines 8 through 12 set up the variables for the `mail()` function.
- Line 13 mails the feedback to the email address specified in line 8.
- Line 14 prints out a "Thank you" to the user for providing feedback on the site.
- If the Submit button was not pushed, lines 15 through 17 escape from PHP and print out the feedback form.
- Lines 18 through 23 print out the feedback form.
- Lines 24 through 26 end the `if/then/else` statement started on line 7.
- Lines 27 and 28 close out the HTML for the page.

◆ Project: Customer Service Feedback Page

The new features you've just learned can really enhance the functionality of your Web site. Now you can open just about any file on your Web server (or from the Web or FTP), and do some processing on it. Additionally, you now have the ability to quickly and easily send email from any of your scripts.

This next project, Script 4-4, takes some of these new features and bundles them together to make a nice customer service utility. Users have the ability to leave three different kinds of feedback.

- Comments on the site and services
- Improvement suggestions
- Complaints

Each of the types of feedback gets posted to a separate Web page, depending on what kind of feedback is given. Also, an email listing the comments from the user is sent to a company email address. And finally, an email is sent to the user to thank them for their feedback. All this in one script and it's only about 50 lines long!

You'll be creating this script for a fictional company called Shelly Biotechnologies. Shelly's corporate Web site contains the latest news on the company's projects and services. Shelly's PR department will be monitoring the Complaints page. The marketing team monitors the comments on the site and services, and the CEO will be monitoring the Improvement Suggestions page to get ideas on how to make her company more customer focused.

Examples of these pages can be seen in Figures 4–8, 4–9, and 4–10.

Script 4-4
customer_service.php3

```
1.  <html>
2.  <head>
3.  <title>Customer Service Form</title></head>
4.  <img src="images/shelly_logo.gif" width=558 height=166
    alt="Shelly Biotechnologies Inc." border="0">
5.  <body bgcolor="#FFFFFF">
6.  <?php
7.  if(isset($submit)):
8.  if($type == "comment"):
9.  $file = "comments.html";
10. elseif($type == "suggestion"):
11. $file = "suggestions.html";
12. else:
13. $file = "complaints.html";
14. endif;
15. if(!$open_file = fopen($file, "a")):
16. print("Error! File can't be opened!");
17. else:
18. $date = date("M d, Y");
19. $comments = "Feedback from $name, $email on $date\n\nTheir
    Feedback is:\n$feedback\n";
20. fwrite($open_file, "<pre>$comments</pre><hr>");
21. fclose($open_file);
```

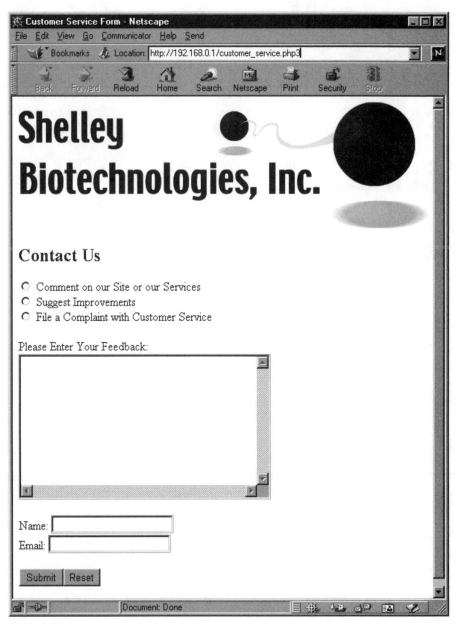

FIGURE 4-8 customer_service.php3

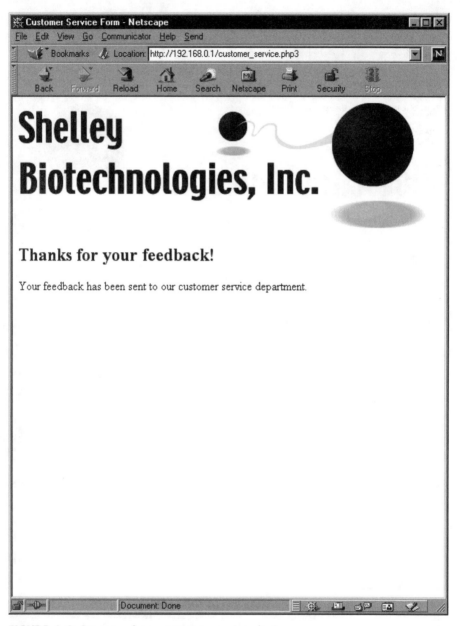

FIGURE 4–9 Response from customer_service.php3

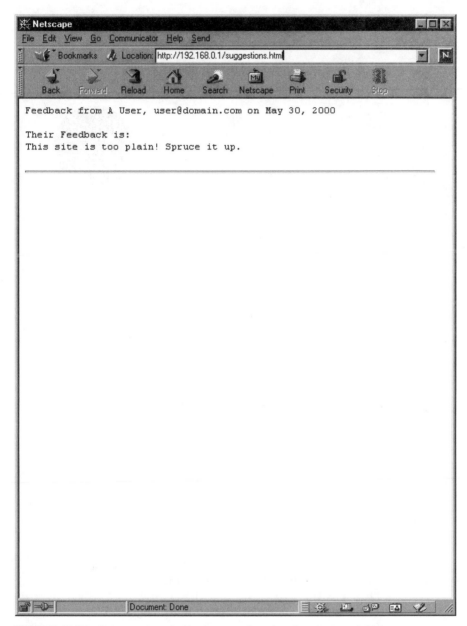

FIGURE 4-10 Comments posted to suggestions.html

```
22. $company_to = "feedback@company.com";
23. $subject1 = "Feedback from the Website!";
24. $subject2 = "Thanks for your feedback!";
25. $body = "Thanks for your recent feedback!\nOur customer
    Service department is looking it over and should get back to
    you shortly.\n";
26. $body .= "\n\nCustomer Service Department";
27. mail($company_to,$subject1,$comments);
28. mail($email,$subject2,$body);
29. ?>
30. <h2>Thanks for your feedback!</h2>
31. <p>Your feedback has been sent to our customer service
    department.
32. <?
33. endif;
34. else:
35. ?>
36. <h2>Contact Us</h2>
37. <form action="customer_service.php3" method="POST">
38. <input type="radio" name="type" value="comment"> Comment on
    our Site or our Services
39. <br><input type="radio" name="type" value="suggestion"> Sug-
    gest Improvements
40. <br><input type="radio" name="type" value="complaint"> File a
    Complaint with Customer Service
41. <p>Please Enter Your Feedback:
42. <br><textarea name="feedback" cols="40" rows="10"></textarea>
43. <p>Name: <input type="text" name="name">
44. <br>Email: <input type="text" name="email">
45. <p><input type="submit" name="submit" value="Submit"><input
    type="Reset">
46. </form>
47. <?
48. endif;
49. ?>
50. </body>
51. </html>
```

HOW THE SCRIPT WORKS

- Lines 1 through 5 are normal HTML.
- Line 6 is the PHP start tag. It tells the Web server to start evaluating the page as PHP rather than as HTML.
- Line 7 checks to see if the Submit button was pressed. If it was, line 8 is executed. If not, line 34 is executed.
- Lines 8 through 13 check to see which radio button in the form was pressed and sets the proper file that the comments should be written to. For example, if the user clicked on the

Comment radio box, then the file that the user's feedback gets written to is comments.html.

- Line 15 attempts to open the file specified in one of the above lines.
- If the file can't be opened, an error message is printed out by line 16.
- Line 17 is the `else` statement that moves on to line 18 if there are no errors opening the file.
- Line 18 generates a date variable to put on the Web page and in the email that gets sent to the company email address.
- At line 19, a string is generated that includes the user's name, email address, and the comments that they submitted. This string is then used in the next line.
- In line 20, the script writes our newly generated string to the file that was opened.
- Line 21 closes the file that was opened.
- On lines 22 through 24 the mail variables are set for the mailings.
- On lines 25 and 26 the script generates the text of a short email message to the customer to thank them for their feedback.
- Lines 27 and 28 send out the emails. One email is sent to the customer with the "Thank you" message. The other email is sent to an employee in the company, telling them the customer's feedback.
- Lines 29 through 32 escape from PHP and print out a short message to the browser, thanking the user for their feedback.
- Line 33 ends the `if/then/else` statement started on line 7.
- Lines 34 through 49 are executed if the Submit button was not pressed. They print the form out to the browser, asking for feedback from the customer.
- Lines 50 and 51 close out the HTML page.

◆ Recap

This chapter has introduced some of the file and string functions in PHP as well as the all powerful (and simple) `mail()` function. This chapter has also shown that you can add some nice features, such as the multifeedback form, to your site with a very few lines of code.

◆ Advanced Projects

1. Read up on Regular Expressions in the PHP Manual at *http://www.php.net/manual/ref.regex.php3.* Regular Expressions allow you to search a string for certain characters or types of characters (and a lot more). Modify Script 4-2 so that it not only checks to see if the proper number of characters are in the zip code, but also that the zip code contains only numbers.

2. Go back to Script 4-4 and modify it so that different email addresses within the company get the feedback based on what kind of feedback was sent. For example, send improvement suggestions to the CEO, send comments on the site to the Webmaster, and send the complaints to PR. You could also modify the email sent to the company so that it references the proper URL for the collection of feedback.

5 Templates and Modularization

IN THIS CHAPTER

- New Functions
- The Power of Modularity
- Project: Modularizing the *Stitch* Web Site

Templates provide an easy way to create many pages with the same structure and layout, but with varying content. Building a Web site based from a template requires modularizing the parts of your site that are similar. This chapter introduces you to some of the concepts of a modular site and gives an example of a highly modular site.

◆ New Functions

include()

```
include( filename );
```

The `include()` function does just what its name sounds like it should do—it includes other files in your script. This is useful so that you can write functions that are used by many different pages, but are kept in just one location. If you need to make changes to the function, you only have to make the one change in an included file, and not across all of your other files. The syntax for the include function is simple.

```
include("file.inc");
```

If you place the above line in one of your scripts, you can use any of the functions in the file *file.inc* in the current script that you are writing. In fact, you can use any of the information, such as variable definitions or HTML snippets, in the included file. You can include almost any type of file, whether it be text, HTML, or PHP. Include files should generally have a *.inc* extension for easy reference.

Include files do not have to be complete PHP[1] or HTML pages. They can be just snippets or fragments of a page. A good example of an include file is navigation links, usually found on the left side of a page. You could create a plain table in HTML for the links, then put just that table into a file to be included in all your other files.

More information on the `include()` function can be found in the PHP manual at *http://www.php.net/manual/html/function.include.html.*

◆ The Power of Modularity

When building a dynamic site, it helps if you create pages that use modular components.

Modular components are small, self-contained objects that make up a bigger object. Think of your Web page as the main object. Within your Web site you have things like navigation bars that are usually the same from page to page across the entire site. You may also have a graphic that is across the top of every page, or a footer containing copyright information across the bottom of every page. All of these items can be turned into a single module and referenced within the rest of your pages.

Modularizing your site gives you a consistent look and feel across the site. If you want to make changes to the site, you only need to make the change in one file and that change is carried throughout the rest of your pages.

---

1. Even though include files don't need to be complete PHP scripts, you should always surround PHP code in your include files with the start and end PHP tags.

◆ Project: Modularizing the *Stitch* Web Site

The next project is an example of a modular site. This is the homepage for the fictional *Stitch* online fashion magazine. The entire page is modularized. The only components of the page that aren't in a module are the page title, headline (Spring!), and content in the middle of the page.

Figure 5–1 shows an example of the main homepage for the *Stitch* site.

Figure 5–2 shows the same page as in Figure 5–1, except that Style Sheet and Graphics have been commented out in the script so that they don't appear on the page. See the results just by commenting out a few lines? Now imagine what you could do if you wanted to redesign your site and it was set up in the same modular fashion as this site. In mere minutes you could have a totally revamped site using the latest cool fonts and graphics.

There are several scripts that make up the template set for the *Stitch* site. Each serves a particular purpose, and some are modules of others. Combined, they make up the framework for the Web site. They are

- **stitch.PAGE.php3**. These are the content pages that pull in all the other pages. Examples are stitch.index.php3 (Script 5-1) and stitch.stolen.php3 (Script 5-8).
- **main.inc** (Script 5-2). This is the main file called in by the PAGE files above.
- **head.inc** (Script 5-3). This page prints out the HTML header information as well as the page title for each of the pages. It also prints out the current date at the top right-hand side of the page and pulls in the *Stitch* logo graphic.
- **style.inc** (Script 5-4). This is the style sheet for the site. It gets called into head.inc for inclusion in the HTML `<head>` area of the main pages.
- **navlinks.inc** (Script 5-5). This file controls the navigation links that appear on the left hand side of the page.
- **search.inc** (Script 5-6). This file controls the Search, Sitemap, and Archives links that appear on the right side of the page.
- **footer.inc** (Script 5-7). This page controls the footer of each page. On this site it just prints out a horizontal rule and copyright information.

FIGURE 5–1 Modular *Stitch* homepage

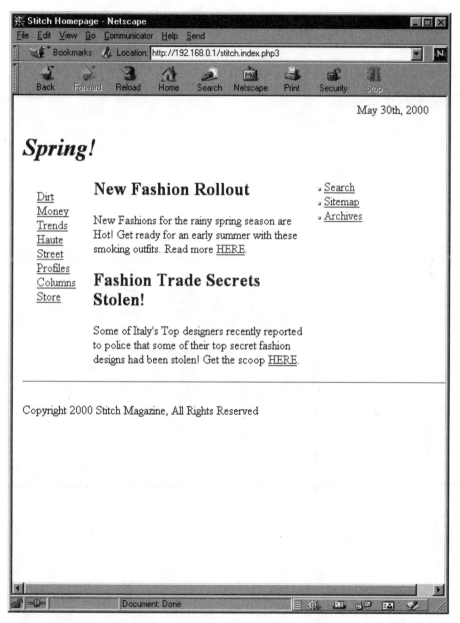

FIGURE 5–2 *Stitch* homepage *sans* Style Sheet and Graphics

Read through all the scripts then consult the following outline for how everything is pulled in, as shown in Figure 5-3.

FIGURE 5-3 An articles from the *Stitch* site

HOW THE TEMPLATES WORK

Step 1. One of the content pages, such as stitch.index.php3, is called from the Web server. The content page specifies three things.

- The title of the page
- The headline for the page
- Content for the page

Step 2. Once these three things are defined, the script calls main.inc, which is the main layout template for the site. It determines where the other include files are displayed on the page. Out of all the files, main.inc includes the most files. The files included in main.inc are

- head.inc
- navlinks.inc
- search.inc
- footer.inc

Additionally, main.inc prints out the contents of the `$content` variable from step 1. The other two variables from step 1, `$title` and `$headline`, are sent to head.inc to be used in the `head()` function. The file head.inc needs to pull in style.inc before it can print its output inside of main.inc.

Step 3. The files search.inc, navlinks.inc, and footer.inc are all printed directly from this file. None of these files need to include other files to be included here. Head.inc prints out the HTML header information (including the `$title`) as well as the current date, the logo that appears at the top of the page, the background image, and the `$headline`. Head.inc calls in style.inc to print out the style sheet.

Script 5-1
stitch.index.php3

```
1.  <?
2.  //You need to specify $title, $headline, and $content
3.  $title = "Stitch Homepage";
4.  $headline = "Spring!";
5.  $content = "
6.  <h2>New Fashion Rollout</h2>
7.  <p>New Fashions for the rainy spring season are Hot!
8.  Get ready for an early summer with these smoking outfits.
9.  Read more <a href=\"#\">HERE</a>.
10. <h2>Fashion Trade Secrets Stolen!</h2>
11. <p>Some of Italy's Top designers recently reported to police
```

```
12. that some of their top secret fashion designs had been stolen!
13. Get the scoop <a href=\"stitch.stolen.php3\">HERE</a>.
14. ";
15. include("main.inc");
16. ?>
```

Script 5-2
main.inc

```
1.  <?
2.  include("head.inc");
3.  head("$title");
4.  ?>
5.  <table width="600">
6.  <tr><td>
7.  <? headline($headline); ?>
8.  <!-- Nav Links -->
9.  <? include("navlinks.inc") ?>
10. <table>
11. <tr><td width="300">
12. <!-- CONTENT goes here -->
13. <? print $content ?>
14. </td>
15. <td valign="TOP">
16. <!-- Search, Sitemap, Archives Links -->
17. <? include("search.inc") ?>
18. </tr></td>
19. </table>
20. </td></tr>
21. <tr><td>
22. <!-- Footer Goes Here -->
23. <? include("footer.inc") ?>
24. </tr></td>
25. </table>
26. </body>
27. </html>
```

Script 5-3
head.inc

```
1.  <?
2.  function head($title) {
3.  ?>
4.  <html>
5.  <head>
6.  <title><? print $title ?></title>
7.  <!-- Style goes here -->
```

```
 8.  <? include("style.inc") ?>
 9.  </head>
10.  <body background="images/stitch_bg.gif">
11.  <div align="RIGHT"><? print date("F jS, Y") ?></div>
12.  <img src="images/stitch_logo.gif" width=516 height=122>
13.  <p>
14.  <?
15.  }
16.  function headline($headline) {
17.  ?>
18.  <h1><i><? print $headline ?></i></h1>
19.  <?
20.  }
21.  ?>
```

Script 5-4
style.inc

```
 1.  <style><!--
 2.  P   {
 3.  font-size : small;}
 4.  H1   {
 5.  font-family : Verdana, Arial;
 6.  text-align : center;
 7.  color : Navy;}
 8.  H2   {
 9.  font-family : Verdana, Arial;
10.  color : Navy;}
11.  H3   {
12.  font-family : Verdana, Arial;}
13.  A   {
14.  color : #302e52;}
15.  A:Visited   {
16.  color : #302e52;}
17.  A:Active   {
18.  color : #302e52;}
19.  BODY   {
20.  font-size : medium;
21.  font-family : Georgia, Times;
22.  color : #302e52;}
23.  A.large   {
24.  font-size : large;
25.  color : #302e52;
26.  font-weight : bold;}
27.  A:Visited.large   {
28.  font-size : large;
29.  color : #302e52;
30.  font-weight : bold;}
```

```
31. A:Active.large  {
32. font-size : large;
33. color : #302e52;
34. font-weight : bold;}
35. P.small  {
36. font-size : x-small;}
37. </style>
```

Script 5-5
navlinks.inc

```
 1. <table cellpadding="15" align="LEFT">
 2. <tr><td>
 3. <a href="#" class="large">Dirt</a><br>
 4. <a href="#" class="large">Money</a><br>
 5. <a href="#" class="large">Trends</a><br>
 6. <a href="#" class="large">Haute</a><br>
 7. <a href="#" class="large">Street</a><br>
 8. <a href="#" class="large">Profiles</a><br>
 9. <a href="#" class="large">Columns</a><br>
10. <a href="#" class="large">Store</a><br>
11. </tr></td>
12. </table>
```

Script 5-6
search.inc

```
1. <img src="images/bullet.gif" width=5 height=5>
   <a href="#">Search</a><br>
2. <img src="images/bullet.gif" width=5 height=5>
   <a href="#">Sitemap</a><br>
3. <img src="images/bullet.gif" width=5 height=5>
   <a href="#">Archives</a>
```

Script 5-7
footer.inc

```
1. <hr size="1" noshade>
2. <p class="small"> Copyright 2000 Stitch Magazine, All Rights
   Reserved</p>
```

Script 5-8
stitch.stolen.php3

```
1. <?
2. //You need to specify $title, $headline, and $content
```

```
 3. $title = "Fashion Designs Stolen!";
 4. $headline = "Fashion Designs Stolen!";
 5. $content = "
 6. <p><b>Milan, Italy</b> - Some disturbing news was announced
    today in Italy.
 7. Some of the biggest designers have recently been the victims
    of so called&quot;
 8. Corporate Espionage.&quot;
 9. <p>Famed designer Antonio Ferarri was quoted as saying
    &quot;It was that guy from
10. America again. He steals our ideas every year. The one with
    the Jeans Commercials.&quot;
11. <p>When asked which of the hundreds of companies in America
    with jeans commercials stole his
12. designs Ferarri replied, &quot;You know who I'm talking about.
    this is an outrage!&quot;
13. Then he stormed out of the interview.
14. <p>Police have no leads yet as to who may have stolen the
    designs.
15. ";
16. include("main.inc");
17. ?>
```

◆ Recap

Creating a modular site *saves time.* Why constantly update multiple files when you can update just one and have your whole site updated in a matter of seconds? Additionally, a modular site is consistent from page to page. If you make a change to your navigation links, they are changed across all the pages that they appear on.

◆ Advanced Project

Play around with the style.inc file and change the appearance of the site. Also, modify the main.inc file to change the layout of the site. Finally try, creating a few of the content files (stitch.index.php3, stitch.stolen.php3) to see how your content fits in with the rest of the page.

6 Dynamically Created Templates

IN THIS CHAPTER

- New Functions
- Dynamic Templates
- Project: The Dynamic Article Page

In the last chapter, "Templates and Modularization," you learned a little about creating a template for a site to greatly reduce the amount of overhead it takes to create a new page. This chapter goes a little further and makes a typical page template into a dynamic page template.

◆ New Functions

strip_tags()

```
$clean_data = strip_tags($tagged_data);
```

The `strip_tags()` function simply strips HTML tags out of a string and returns the same string *sans* the HTML tags.

More information on the `strip_tags()` function can be found on the PHP Web site at *http://www.php.net/manual/html/function.strip-tags.html.*

◆ Dynamic Templates

Different users have different needs for the same kind of information. Some users are perfectly happy with viewing your content online in a Web browser. Other users want to print out the information. And yet other users like to email certain information to their friends or coworkers. Some users also like to do all three of these things at one time or another. With a dynamic template, you can easily reformat your information to fit all of these particular needs.

◆ Project: The Dynamic Article Page

This next project, Script 6-1, teaches you how to create a dynamic template for a page that can format the content into three formats: Web, print, and email. You need to create your content only once; then the template formats the article based on what the user wants. Examples of these pages can be seen in Figures 6–1, 6–2, 6–3, and 6–4.

This template can be used for any article. All articles are written in a separate file, using normal HTML, but the HTML, HEAD, and BODY tags are left out of the article file.

The filename must be referenced in the URL for the script to work correctly. By default the script looks in the same directory for any files that need to be displayed. The example article file used in this script is called *article1.html*. To view the file from a browser, the user would need to go to this URL:

```
http://servername.com/dynamic_template.php3?article=article1.html
```

Script 6-1
dynamic_template.php3

```
1.  <html>
2.  <head>
3.     <title>The Dynamic Article</title>
4.  </head>
5.  <body>
6.  <?
7.
8.  if(isset($format)):
9.     if($format == "print"):
10.           $file = fopen($article, "r");
```

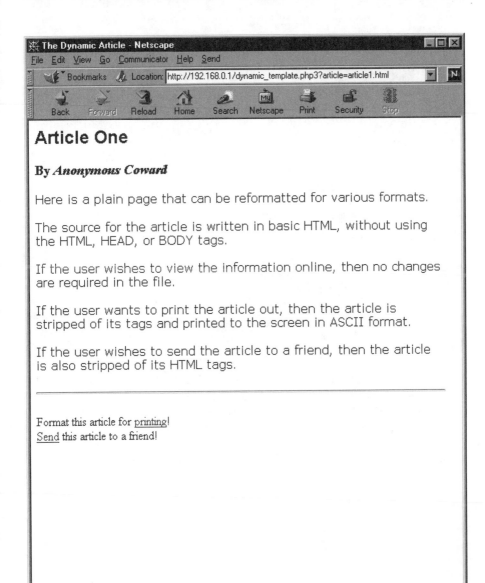

FIGURE 6-1 Article page, normal view

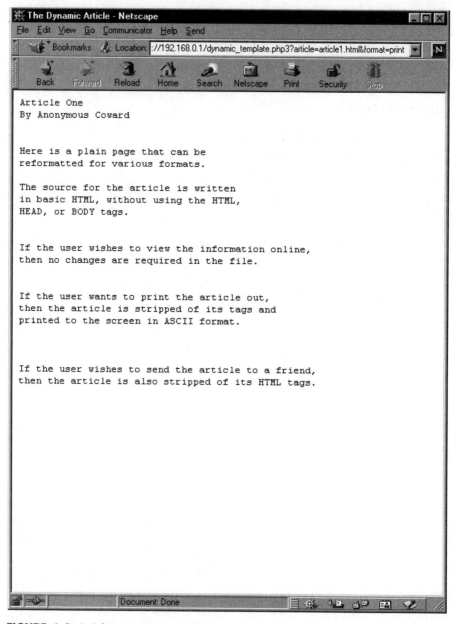

FIGURE 6-2 Article page, Print It view

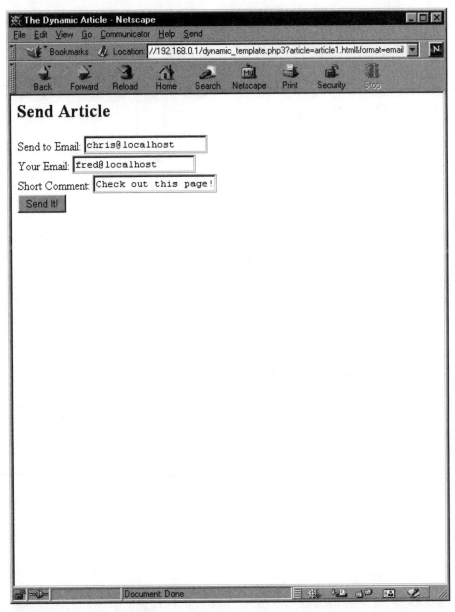

FIGURE 6–3 Article page, Email to Friend form

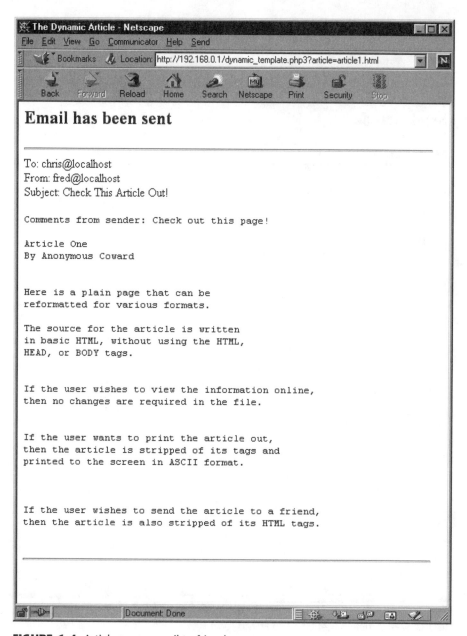

FIGURE 6–4 Article page, email to friend

```
11.            $data = fread($file, 1000);
12.            fclose($file);
13.            $stripped_data = strip_tags($data);
14.            print("<pre>$stripped_data</pre>");
15.     elseif($format == "email"):
16.            ?>
17.            <h2>Send Article</h2>
18.            <form action="dynamic_template.php3" method="POST">
19.            <p>Send to Email: <input type="text" name="to">
20.            <br>Your Email: <input type="text" name="from">
21.            <br>Short Comment: <input type="text"
    name="comment">
22.            <input type="hidden" name="article" value="<? echo
    $article ?>">
23.            <br><input type="submit" name="submit" value="Send
    It!">
24.            </form>
25.            <?
26.     endif;
27. elseif(isset($submit)):
28.     $file = fopen($article, "r");
29.     $data = fread($file, 1000);
30.     fclose($file);
31.     $stripped_data = strip_tags($data);
32.     $body = "Comments from sender: " . $comment . "\n\n" .
    $stripped_data;
33.     $subject = "Check This Article Out!";
34.     mail($to, $subject, $body, "FROM: $from");
35.     ?>
36.     <h2>Email has been sent</h2>
37.     <hr>
38.     <?
39.     print("To: $to<br>From: $from<br>Subject:
    $subject<p><pre>$body</pre><hr>\n");
40.
41. else:
42.     $file = fopen($article, "r");
43.     $data = fread($file, 1000);
44.     fclose($file);
45.     print("$data");
46.     ?>
47.     <hr>
48.     <p>Format this article for
    <a href="dynamic_template.php3?article=<? echo $article ?>
    &format=print">printing</a>!
49.     <br><a href="dynamic_template.php3?article=<? echo $article
    ?>&format=email">Send</a> this article to a friend!
50.     <?
```

```
51. endif;
52.
53. ?>
54. </body>
55. </html>
```

HOW THE SCRIPT WORKS

- Lines 1 through 5 are normal HTML.
- Line 6 is the trusty PHP start tag.
- Line 8 checks to see if the format variable has been set in the URL. If it is set to print, then the script executes lines 10 through 14. If it is not set to print, then line 15 is executed.
- Lines 10 through 14 should look familiar to you. They are almost the same as the file_read.php3 script in Chapter 4 "Files, Strings, and Mail." These lines are executed only if the format variable has been set to print in the URL of the script.
- Lines 15 through 25 are executed if the format variable has been set to email. A form is printed to the screen, asking the user for their email address, the recipient's email address, and any short comments they want to add to the article.
- After the user presses the Submit button, the script executes lines 27 through 40.
- These lines are executed if the user requested to send the article to a friend. The article is read into the script and any HTML tags in the article file are stripped out using the strip_tags() function. After the tags are stripped out, a mail message is sent using the email addresses provided by the user, and the script also includes any comments the user may have added. Finally, the text of the email, as well as a short confirmation message telling the user that the email was sent, is printed to the screen.
- Lines 41 through 51 are executed as the default mode of viewing the page. The article file is simply read into the script and printed out to the screen as it was written. Additionally, two links are provided on the bottom of the page, allowing the user to view the page as a print format, or allowing the user to send the article to a friend.
- Line 53 is the trusty close PHP tag.
- Lines 54 and 55 close out the HTML for the page.

Script 6-2
article.html

```
1.  <h2><FONT face=Arial>Article One</FONT> </h2>
2.  <h3>By <EM>Anonymous Coward</EM>  </h3>
3.  <p><FONT face=Verdana>Here is a plain page that can be
4.  reformatted for various formats. </FONT>
5.  <p><FONT face=Verdana>The source for the article is written
6.  in basic HTML, without using the HTML, HEAD, or BODY tags.
    </FONT>
7.  <p><FONT face=Verdana>If the user wishes to view the
8.  information online, then no changes are required in the file.
    </FONT>
9.  <p><FONT face=Verdana>If the user wants to print the
10. article out, then the article is stripped of its tags and
    printed to the screen
11. in ASCII format. </FONT>
12. <p><FONT face=Verdana>If the user wishes to send the
13. article to a friend then the article is also stripped of its
    HTML tags.
14. </FONT></p>
```

ABOUT SCRIPT 6-2

Script 6-2, *article.html,* is simple HTML. It's important to write the page with hard returns in the correct places, since that will be how the page is viewed in the *print it* and *email* modes.

A good rule of thumb for creating a page that is to be included in a template such as this is to write the article in ASCII text first and make sure the formatting is correct. Then go back and add HTML tags, such as headings, font, and paragraph tags. That way you can always be sure the page is formatted correctly in its plain form.

◆ Recap

This chapter showed some simple examples of creating a dynamic template that changes to accommodate a user's needs.

◆ Advanced Project

Web sites that offer "Print this Page" types of options usually have very busy content pages. There are banner ads and navigation links on each side of the content, or sometimes the data is in a table that doesn't print out correctly. The example in this chapter was quite simple and maybe didn't require a separate function to format the page for printing. Add some navigation bars, banner ads, and other eye-catching content to the default view of the page, but do not include it in the *print it* or *email* modes of the page.

There is also one problem with this script: if a user tries to call the script with no argument, such as by just calling *http://localhost\dynamic_template.php3,* then the script generates an error. Create a default page view that appears if a clever user tries to call the script from his or her browser in this manner.

7 Let the Data Drive

◆ Good Things Come in Free Packages

Data-driven Web sites—you've heard the term thrown about the local Starbucks® a million times, spoken by men and women with really nice shoes and really small laptops. You've heard about the power of Microsoft's® Active Server Pages™, and of the awe and might of Allaire's® Cold Fusion. But you think to yourself, *We don't have any more money in the budget; there's no way we can afford one of those commercial databases or application servers. Besides that, who's going to develop it? The developer alone is out of our price range.*

Luckily, you can do it yourself using tools that are easier to use and can produce the same results as expensive commercial applications can give you. In this chapter you'll be introduced to the free[1] MySQL database and shown how to use it with PHP to create your own data-driven Web sites.

Integrating your Web site with a database opens up worlds of possible features that you can add to give your users a more interactive and robust experience while visiting your site. It also makes it easier for you, as a developer, to create a site by using modularized pieces of information stored in a database.

If you did the earlier projects (and I know you did—you wouldn't skip ahead would you?), you can easily use PHP to connect to a database and join in on the data-driven Web site frenzy.

◆ New Functions

printf()

printf() is basically the same as print(), only it gives you a little more precision as to how you want to format the display of your variables. In the following example, the %s is replaced by the variables at the end of the statement. The %s tells the printf function to format the variables as strings, as opposed to, say, an integer or binary number.

```
printf("<TR><TD>%s</TD><TD>%s</TD></TR>\n", $row["col1"],
$row["col2"]);
```

while

The while statement is a simple looping mechanism that allows you to evaluate a set of data until it comes across a value that doesn't meet the required criteria. The loop is exited once the evaluation against the criteria is proven false. This function is useful if you don't know the size of the data set you need to evaluate—for instance, some data retrieved from a database.

```
while($a == $b) {

    print("<P> $a is equal to $b \n");

}
```

---

1. See the License Information that comes with MySQL for full details. A MySQL license must be purchased for Windows™ servers after a 30-day trial period. There are some additional license restrictions for commercial repackaging of MySQL.

mysql_connect

The `mysql_connect` function establishes a connection with a MySQL Server. It takes as its arguments the MySQL server location, your MySQL login, and your MySQL password.

This function is usually assigned to a variable that is then used in the `mysql_select_db` function.

```
$server_connection = mysql_connect("localhost", "chris",
"password1");
```

NOTE:
The password argument is necessary only if you have set a MySQL password for yourself. If you don't have a password, and don't need one to connect to the server, you can leave the password argument out of the function.

mysql_select_db

The `mysql_select_db` function selects a particular MySQL database on a MySQL server. It takes as its arguments the database name and the MySQL server connection. You must use this function to select a database on the server before you can send queries.

```
mysql_select_db("news", "$server_connection");
```

mysql_query

The `mysql_query` function sends SQL queries to a database on a MySQL server. It takes as its argument an SQL query. If you are connecting to more than one MySQL server in a script, then you can specify which connection you want to query by adding a server connection to the arguments.

```
$result = mysql_query("SELECT * FROM news");

$result = mysql_query("SELECT * FROM news",
"$server_connection");
```

mysql_fetch_array

The `mysql_fetch_array` function takes the first row of the result of a MySQL query and puts it into an array. Each call to this function gets the next row of the data from the result of the query until no rows are left. Either the column number or the column name can reference the array.

```
$myrow = mysql_fetch_array($result);
```

◆ Installing MySQL

Installing MySQL is fairly straightforward for both Windows and Linux. You can get the latest versions of MySQL from *http://www .mysql.com/download.html*. From there, click on the appropriate download link for your operating system.

If you are using Windows 95/98 or NT, download the latest shareware version. You'll need to fill out a short registration questionnaire before you can download the setup program.

Once you have downloaded the shareware version, extract the zip file and execute the *setup.exe* program. The setup program should install the MySQL files in C:\mysql.

Then all you need to do is start the MySQL server daemon by executing the command *C:\mysql\mysqld –install*. Subsequently, you can start the MySQL server daemon by issuing the command *C:\mysql\mysqld*. Remember that the MySQL server daemon must be running if you want to connect to your databases using PHP.

If you are using a flavor of Linux that supports Red Hat's RPM format, I strongly recommend downloading one of the RPM binary versions of the latest stable release of MySQL. The RPM versions install all the necessary startup scripts, and generally take a lot of the headaches out of compiling your own binary version from the source code.

To install the RPM version of MySQL just issue the command *rpm –ivh <MYSQL-RPM>.rpm,* where <MYSQL-RPM> is the name of the MySQL RPM package that you downloaded. This package automatically installs the startup scripts and configures the default databases.

As always, be sure to read the installation documentation that is available on the MySQL Web site for more detailed information.

◆ Setting up PHP to Work with MySQL

After you have installed MySQL, you'll need to make a few minor adjustments to your PHP installation before the two programs will play nice with each other. For Windows users, this means you need to make one small change to your .ini file. For Linux users, this means that you'll have to recompile PHP once again.

If you are using the Windows version of PHP, you need to edit the *php3.ini* file (or *php.ini* if you are using PHP4) in C:\windows or C:\WINNT, depending on your operating system.

To enable PHP to work with MySQL, you need to uncomment the line that says "extension=php3_mysql.dll." To do this you need to delete the semicolon from in front of that line. The line should look like the one below.

```
;Windows Extensions
extension=php3_mysql.dll
```

Now save the file and restart your Apache server, and you are all set to go.

If you are using Linux, you need to recompile your version of PHP. While this may take a few more minutes to set up than if you were using Windows, you'll once again have the satisfaction of turning a bunch of source code into a living, breathing program. After all, that's why you are a Linux user!

When you recompile, just follow the same steps you used in Chapter 1, only add the flag—with-mysql when you issue the configure command. This tells the PHP compile program to include the extra functions you'll need when connecting to the database.

After that, you'll need to stop and restart your Apache server for the changes to take effect.

◆ SQL Queries

SQL (Structured Query Language) is a powerful, robust, and sometimes complicated query language that lets you manipulate information in databases. Luckily, you can get by at first with only the most basic knowledge of the SQL language to use it effectively in PHP. Table 7.1 lists some of the most frequently used commands. In the usage examples, news is the name of the table, and news_id is the name of a column in the table.

In general, it's good SQL programming practice to capitalize the SQL language keywords, such as SELECT, WHERE, and UPDATE. This makes your SQL queries easier to read, and easier for other programmers to look at your code and understand what is going on.

TABLE 7.1 SQL Basics

Keyword	Definition and Usage
SELECT	Used to select data from the database. The data that you select is put into a table. **Usage** `SELECT * FROM news WHERE news_id > '1'`
INSERT	Used to insert new information into the database. **Usage** `INSERT INTO news VALUES(NULL,'1','10-22-2000','Chris')`
DELETE	Used to delete a row of data from a database. **Usage** `DELETE FROM news WHERE news_id = '5'`
UPDATE	Used to modify data in the database. **Usage** `UPDATE news SET urgent = 'YES' WHERE news_id = '5'`

◆ Setting up a Simple Database

First you need to create a database to store your data. Make certain you have your MySQL daemon running. Replace DBNAME with whatever name you want to name your database. If you are using Windows, you need to execute any MySQL commands from C:\mysql\bin. For Linux, you can issue the commands from any shell prompt. To create your database, issue the following command:

```
prompt>mysqladmin create DBNAME
```

To set up the tables in your new database, you need to login to your MySQL server. This is done by using the MySQL command-line interface.

1. At the prompt, issue the following command:

```
prompt> mysql -u root
```

This command logs you into the server. From here you can create tables, delete (drop) tables, and modify the data in your tables. But first, you must specify which database on the server you want to use, since the MySQL server is capable of hosting multiple databases.

2. At the MySQL prompt, enter the following command and be sure to replace DBNAME with your database's name.

```
mysql> use DBNAME;
```

The MySQL server responds with:

```
Database changed
```

You've now selected your database. Any of the basic SQL queries you enter are directed to this database.

3. Now you can create the table you'll be using for the up-coming projects. Enter the following commands at the MySQL prompt. Hit **Enter** after each line. MySQL doesn't try to interpret the commands until it sees a semicolon (;), so the command itself isn't really executed on the server until you enter the last line.

```
mysql> CREATE TABLE news (
    -> news_id INT NOT NULL AUTO_INCREMENT,
    -> heading VARCHAR(48),
    -> body TEXT,
    -> date DATE,
    -> author_name VARCHAR(48),
    -> author_email VARCHAR(48),
    -> PRIMARY KEY(news_id));
```

If the server gives you a big **ERROR** and spits out a bunch of garbage at you, just try again from the top. You need to enter each line in the sequence from the beginning, exactly as shown.

NOTE:
The → prompt you see after entering a line in the MySQL server is telling you that it's waiting for more input before it does anything.

The server responds with:

```
Query OK, 0 rows affected (0.00 sec)
```

Congratulations! You've just created your first table in MySQL.

◆ Basic SQL Queries

Now that you've set up your first table, you can practice some of the basic SQL queries using the command-line interface of the MySQL server. These exercises will help you get comfortable with basic SQL queries.

First, let's talk about the structure of your new table before we start entering data into it. If you want to see the structure of a particular table, you can ask MySQL to describe it by simply issuing the command `describe`.

Type:

```
mysql> describe news;
```

and the server displays the description of your `news` table

```
+--------------+--------------+------+-----+---------+----------------+
| Field        | Type         | Null | Key | Default | Extra          |
+--------------+--------------+------+-----+---------+----------------+
| news_id      | int(11)      |      | PRI | 0       | auto_increment |
| heading      | varchar(48)  | YES  |     | NULL    |                |
| body         | text         | YES  |     | NULL    |                |
| date         | date         | YES  |     | NULL    |                |
| author_name  | varchar(48)  | YES  |     | NULL    |                |
| author_email | varchar(48)  | YES  |     | NULL    |                |
+--------------+--------------+------+-----+---------+----------------+
6 rows in set (0.00 sec)
```

The table that MySQL returns from the `describe` command gives you all the relevant details of your table.

Here is a brief explanation of the output from the `describe` command:

- Each of the `Field`s holds your data.
- The `Type` of field is what kind of data that particular field can hold.
- If the field has `YES` in its `Null` column, then it can be empty for any row on the table.
- If the field has `PRI` in the `Key` column, then that field acts as an index of sorts for the table. No two values can be the same in any row of a table that is the primary key.
- The `Default` column describes what values, by default, are entered into the field.
- Finally, the `Extra` column describes any extra attributes a row might have, such as `auto_increment`, which increments your primary key by 1 every time you add a new row into the table.

Inserting Data

Now, let's put some data into your new table. Type in the following code at the MySQL prompt. Remember to hit enter at the end of each line.

```
mysql> INSERT INTO news
        -> VALUES(NULL,'A Heading','The Body',
        -> '08-16-2000','Chris C.',
        -> 'chris@domain.com');
```

The server responds with:

```
Query OK, 1 row affected (0.00 sec)
```

Now let's query the database and see how it looks in the table by issuing a `select` statement. The * operator works just like a standard UNIX wildcard.

Type the following at the MySQL prompt:

```
mysql> select * from news;
```

The server responds with:

```
+---------+-----------+----------+------------+-------------+------------------+
| news_id | heading   | body     | date       | author_name | author_email     |
+---------+-----------+----------+------------+-------------+------------------+
|       1 | A Heading | The Body | 0000-00-00 | Chris C.    | chris@domain.com |
+---------+-----------+----------+------------+-------------+------------------+
1 row in set (0.06 sec)
```

Modifying Data

Now what if you entered something incorrectly and you want to modify it? Let's look at the above output. Notice anything strange? The date is listed as 0000-00-00. And no, that isn't some kind of Y2K bug. It's because we didn't enter the date into the table using the correct format. We tried to enter it as *08-16-2000* when we should have entered *2000-08-16*. The date type of data in MySQL won't accept a value that doesn't fit the required parameters. The required parameters state that the date must be a four-digit year, followed by a dash, followed by a two-digit month, followed by a dash, followed by a two-digit day.

To correct the error, you can issue the `update` command. Type the following at the MySQL prompt:

```
mysql> update news set date='2000-08-16' where news_id='1';
```

The server responds:

```
Query OK, 1 row affected (0.00 sec)
```

Just to make sure everything is correct, let's issue the `select` command again. Type the following at the MySQL prompt:

```
mysql> select * from news;
```

The server responds:

```
+---------+-----------+----------+------------+-------------+------------------+
| news_id | heading   | body     | date       | author_name | author_email     |
+---------+-----------+----------+------------+-------------+------------------+
|       1 | A Heading | The Body | 2000-08-16 | Chris C.    | chris@domain.com |
+---------+-----------+----------+------------+-------------+------------------+
1 row in set (0.06 sec)
```

And as you can see from the output, the date is now entered correctly.

Deleting Data

Now that you have learned how to insert, retrieve, and modify data in your database, the last basic command you need to know is the `delete` command.

To delete a row in your table, type this command at the MySQL prompt:

```
mysql> delete from news where news_id='1';
```

The server responds:

```
Query OK, 1 row affected (0.00 sec)
```

Now do a select statement and see what the table looks like.

```
mysql> select * from news;
```

The server responds with:

```
Empty set (0.00 sec)
```

MySQL returns "Empty set" because the criteria you used for the `select` statement (the * operator) returned no values, so this table is empty. If you had used some form of criteria, such as `select * from news where news_id='5'`, an empty set might also be returned, but there could still be data in the table. For example, the table could still contain data where `news_id` equals 2, or 3, or 4. But since you asked for everything in the table, and nothing was returned, you know the table is empty.

The `delete` command simply deletes a row (or rows) that meets the criteria. In this case you deleted the row from your table that had a `news_id` of 1. You could have also chosen to delete rows that had an `author_name` of Chris C., which could delete multiple rows. If the data had hundreds of rows, we could delete them all by using a command such as `delete from news where news_id > '0';`.

◆ Putting Content into Your Database with PHP

Now that you have had a little experience using SQL queries from the MySQL command line, let's try some queries using PHP. Using PHP for the task is less cumbersome, more flexible, and above all, it can easily be done using a Web browser.

The logic behind PHP and database interaction is simple.

- Connect to the database server and login.
- Choose the database to use.
- Send SQL queries to the server to add, delete, and modify data.

You don't even have to worry about closing the connection to the server because PHP does it for you.

Script 7-1 shows you just how easy it is to put data into a database. What PHP allows you to do in a few short, simple lines is amazing. This script uses the `news` MySQL table that you created earlier. If you haven't done so, you need to create it now. Out of the thirty lines of code in the script, there are only about ten that are PHP-specific. The rest is plain HTML. Examples are shown in Figures 7–1 and 7–2.

Script 7-1
data_in.php3

```
1.  <html>
2.  <head>
3.  <title>Putting Data in the Database</title>
4.  </head>
5.  <body bgcolor="#FFFFFF">
6.  <?php
7.  /* This program enters news items into a database */
8.  if(isset($submit)):
9.  $db = mysql_connect("localhost", "root");
```

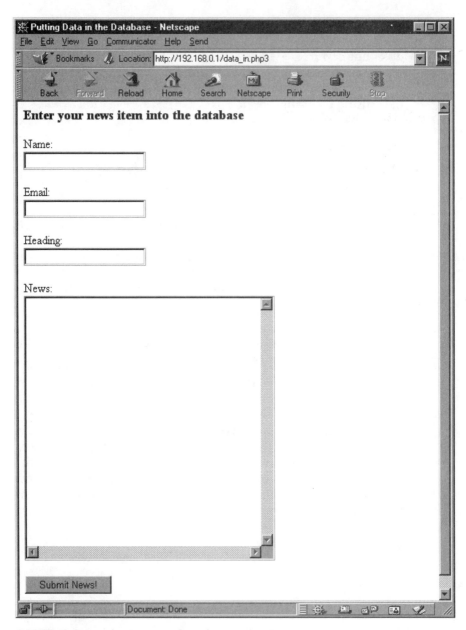

FIGURE 7–1 Initial news entry form from Script 7-1

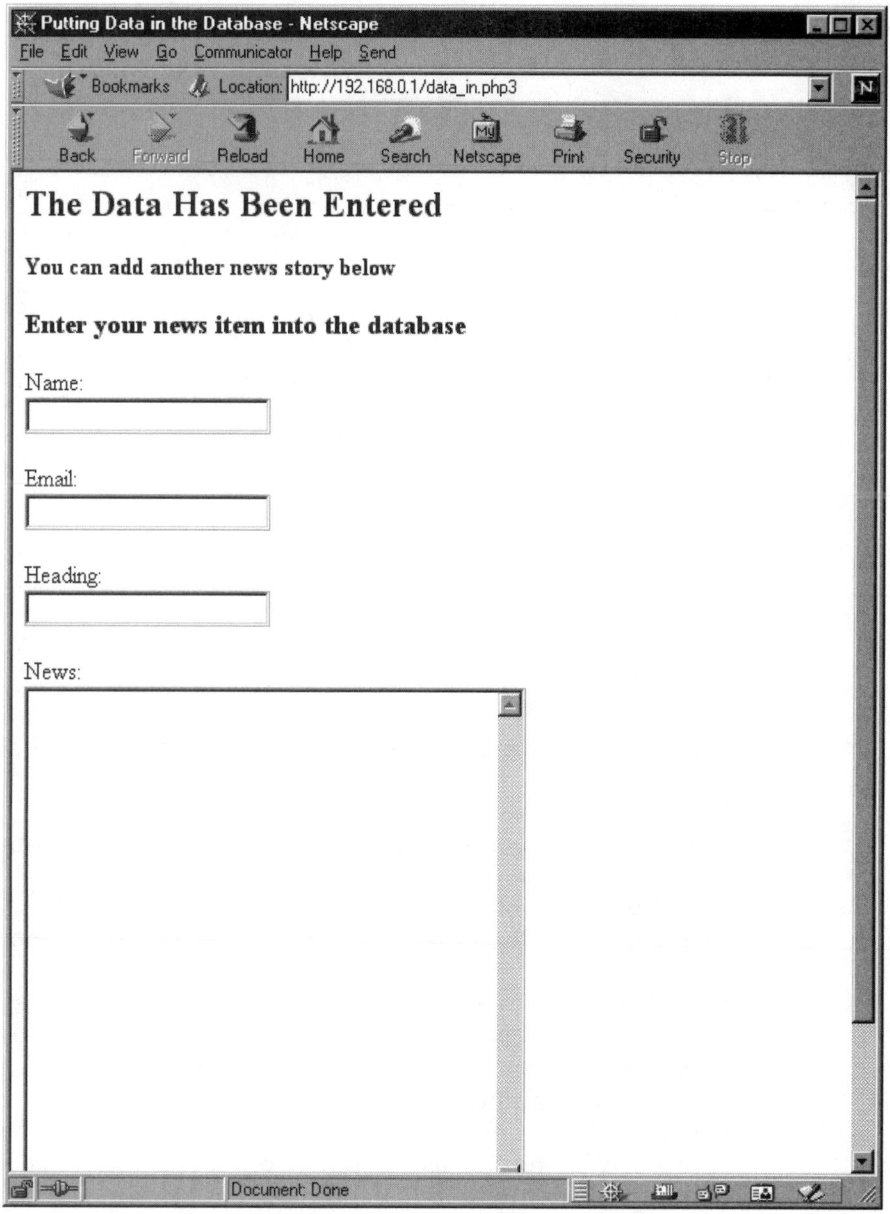

FIGURE 7-2 Result of the form submission from Script 7-1

```
10.  mysql_select_db("php3", $db);
11.  $date = date("Y-m-d");
12.  $sql = "INSERT INTO news
13.  VALUES(NULL,'$heading','$body','$date',
     '$auth','$auth_email')";
14.  mysql_query($sql);
15.  print("<h2>The Data Has Been Entered</h2>\n");
16.  print("<b>You can add another news story below</b><hr>\n");
17.  endif;
18.  ?>
19.  <p><h3>Enter your news item into the database</h3>
20.  <form action="data_in.php3" method="post">
21.  Name:<br><input type="text" name="auth"><p>
22.  Email:<br> <input type="text" name="auth_email"><p>
23.  Heading:<br><input type="text" name="heading"><p>
24.  News:<br>
25.  <textarea cols=40 rows=20 name="body" wrap="virtual">
26.  </textarea><p>
27.  <input type="submit" name="submit" value="Submit News!">
28.  </form>
29.  </body>
30.  </html>
```

HOW THE SCRIPT WORKS

- Line 8 checks to see if the Submit button has been pressed. If it has, it executes the code. If not, it skips to the endif part of the script. In this script, if the button isn't pressed, the PHP code is almost completely ignored. This makes for faster initial loading of the page.
- Line 9 is a variable is assigned to the mysql_connect function. This variable is used in the next line to actually establish the connection. The arguments for the function tell the script to connect to the MySQL server running on localhost, and to login to it with a username of root. This particular server doesn't require a password, so it has not been included as an argument to the function.
- Line 10 calls the function mysql_select_db, which selects the database you want to use, and it also initiates the connection to the server by calling the value of the $db variable.
- Line 12 is the SQL statement. In this case the statement is assigned to a variable so that the mysql_query is easier to read.
- Line 14, the mysql_query function, sends the SQL statement to the MySQL server. The SQL statement that is being sent

tells the MySQL server to enter the values it received from the form into the database table. Here the script also prints out a message letting the user know that his or her data was entered.

- Line 19 returns to plain old HTML. The beauty of this script is that there isn't a lot of overhead. It lets PHP do the hard stuff, and lets HTML do the rest. We could have created a function to print the form to the browser, but that would just put more work on the server because it would have to process more PHP directives. With this script, we keep things simple, fast, and efficient.

The script also repeats itself so that multiple news items can be entered in one session. The HTML form gets printed out every time the script is run, and every time the user hits Submit more data is entered into the database.

Now, of course, this is an ultra-simple example. You would want to include the error-checking statements you learned earlier in the book, and you would also want to spice it up a little and make it easier for the eyes of your users by using a simple style sheet.

◆ Getting Content out of Your Database with PHP

OK, so you've got your PHP scripts set up to put as much data as you want into the database. Now what? Well, you could always go back to that not-so-user-friendly command-line interface that MySQL offers you and do `select` statements all day and night to see what's in there, or you could do it the easy way with PHP.

The basic PHP/MySQL logic is still the same to get data out of the database. You connect to the database server and login; choose the database to use; send SQL queries to the server to add, delete, and modify data—*voila.*

This script also introduces you to the `while` statement. You'll use the `while` statement because it's not always definite how much data your SQL queries will return. You may get one row of data from a query, or you might get fifty. The `while` statement lets you go through all the data returned from your query, then stops when the data ends. Examples of this are shown in Figures 7–3, 7–4, and 7–5.

FIGURE 7–3 Initial load of Script 7-2

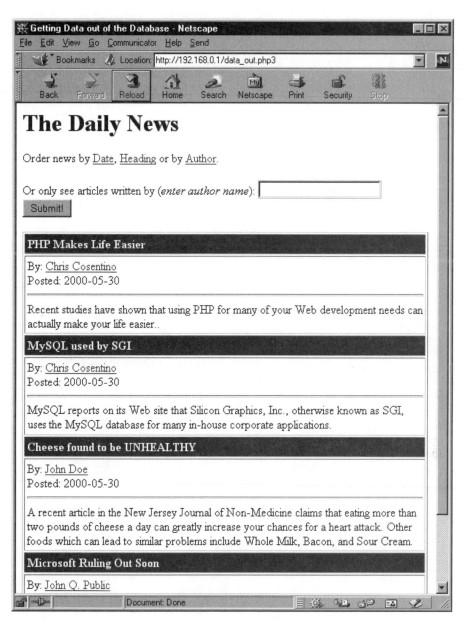

FIGURE 7-4   Script 7-2 after clicking on the Order by Author link

FIGURE 7–5 Script 7-2 displaying articles by author

Since the basic concepts are the same, we'll spice up Script 7-2, with a few extra features to enhance the user's viewing experience. We'll give the user the choice of how he or she wants the information ordered, and we'll also give the user the choice of which author's articles he or she wants to view.

Script 7-2
data_out.php3

```
1.  <html>
2.  <head>
3.  <title>Getting Data out of the Database</title>
4.  </head>
5.  <body bgcolor="#FFFFFF">
6.  <h1>The Daily News</h1>
7.  Order news by
8.  <a href="data_out.php3?orderby=date">Date</a>,
9.  <a href="data_out.php3?orderby=heading">Heading</a> or by
10. <a href="data_out.php3?orderby=author">Author</a>.
11. <p>
12. <form action="data_out.php3" method="POST">
13. Or only see articles written by (<i>enter author name</i>):
14. <input type="text" name="author">
15. <input type="submit" name="submit" value="Submit!">
16. </form>
17. <table border="1" cellpadding="3">
18. <?php
19. /* This program gets news items from the database */
20. $db = mysql_connect("localhost", "root");
21. mysql_select_db("php3", $db);
22. if ($orderby == 'date'):
23. $sql = "select * from news order by 'date'";
24. elseif ($orderby == 'author'):
25. $sql = "select * from news order by 'author_name'";
26. elseif ($orderby == 'heading'):
27. $sql = "select * from news order by 'heading'";
28. elseif (isset($submit)):
29. $sql = "select * from news where author_name = '$author'";
30. else:
31. $sql = "select * from news";
32. endif;
33. $result = mysql_query($sql);
34. while ($row = mysql_fetch_array($result)) {
35. print("<tr><td bgcolor=\"#003399\"><b>");
36. printf("<font color=\"white\">%s</font></b></td></tr>\n",
37. $row["heading"]);
38. printf("<td>By: <a href=\"mailto:%s\">%s</a>\n",
```

```
39. $row["author_email"], $row["author_name"]);
40. printf("<br>Posted: %s<hr>\n",
41. $row["date"]);
42. printf("%s</td></tr>\n",
43. $row["body"]);
44. }
45. ?>
46. </table>
47. </body>
48. </html>
```

HOW THE SCRIPT WORKS

- As you remember from previous chapters in the book, these URLs send variables to PHP. The variables in lines 8 through 10 are used by the PHP script to determine which SQL statements it will send to the MySQL server.
- The form in lines 12 through 16 is used to send an optional query to show only those news items written by a single author. No values are returned if the user enters an author name that is not in the database.
- Lines 20 and 21 establish the connection to the MySQL server and select the database that is used for the queries.
- Lines 22 through 32 give the users some power over what kind of information they can get out of the database and how this information is displayed. The links in lines 8 through 10 and the form in lines 12 through 16 determine which of the if statements are used. The orderby variable drives how the data is displayed. If the orderby variable has no value and the Submit button was not pressed, then line 31 is used as the SQL query.
- At line 33, the query must be done and the data is stored in $result.
- At line 34, the mysql_fetch_array function grabs a row of all the data returned from the query. The while statement increments the row after each loop. The loop continues until all the rows returned from the query are processed by the mysql_fetch_array function.
- With lines 35 through 43, each of the rows returned by the mysql_fetch_array function are printed out using the printf function. The columns of each row are referenced by their column name.
- At line 44, the while loop ends after all the rows returned from the SQL query are processed.

◆ Recap

The database lets you modularize your data into convenient chunks of information that are easy to manage, and it makes it easy for the users to get at the information they want.

Database integration with your Web site gives you a lot of flexibility on how you can display information. We could have done the same thing by writing the output of the data_in script to a text file. But if you did that, you couldn't selectively display only certain authors, nor could you change the order of the display. Now imagine that there were 1,000 news items to sort through. One large text file containing all that information would make it difficult for users to get at the information that they want.

But the best part is, database integration using PHP is quick and easy. As you saw in Script 7-1, it takes only a few lines of basic code to use a database with PHP.

8

chapter

More Robust Data-Driven Applications

IN THIS CHAPTER

- Using Multiple Data Tables
- User Authentication
- Project: Creating a Mini Slashdot for the *Stitch* Site

You've only just brushed the tip of the iceberg in the world of data-driven applications, but the techniques you have learned up to this point can take you much further.

◆ Using Multiple Data Tables

In the examples in Chapter 7, "Let the Data Drive," you used only one table to store the data for your application. As your Web applications get more complex, you need to use multiple tables for several reasons. The main reason is that using only one table makes your data rather unwieldy. The data becomes difficult to manage, and it also makes it difficult to modify data if you want to add new fields.

In designing relational databases, there is a basic rule called *rationalization*. Rationalization basically means that all data in the fields of any particular table should be unique. There should never be an instance where the data is exactly the same in any given field of any particular table. If it turns out that the data in any given field might be the same, then those fields should be

121

taken out of the table and put into a new table. The data from the new table should then be referenced into the primary table in the database.

Let's take a look at the MySQL table used for the scripts in Chapter 7.

```
+--------------+-------------+------+-----+---------+----------------+
| Field        | Type        | Null | Key | Default | Extra          |
+--------------+-------------+------+-----+---------+----------------+
| news_id      | int(11)     |      | PRI | 0       | auto_increment |
| heading      | varchar(48) | YES  |     | NULL    |                |
| body         | text        | YES  |     | NULL    |                |
| date         | date        | YES  |     | NULL    |                |
| author_name  | varchar(48) | YES  |     | NULL    |                |
| author_email | varchar(48) | YES  |     | NULL    |                |
+--------------+-------------+------+-----+---------+----------------+
```

Now think about the kind of information that goes into each of the fields of the table and try to determine which fields are likely to have duplicate information throughout several rows of data. The fields that come to mind immediately are author_name, and author_email.

These fields are likely to repeat because there are generally only a few authors on staff who write lots of articles, and the authors probably use only a single email associated with the site for which they are writing articles.

The headings and bodies of the news articles are more likely not to repeat. It's almost certain that each of the headlines and articles will be unique because, let's face it, the same news stories over and over again probably won't attract many readers to your site.

The big dilemma of storing all your data in one table is simple: What happens when one of those repeating fields changes? If an author changed his or her name, say through marriage or some other scandal, or changed his or her email, you'd have to go through and change each instance of that author's name or email throughout the whole database. If there were thousands of articles in the database, hundreds of which were written by a single author, then changing all that data becomes wildly inefficient and bothersome.

But if that repeating data was put into a separate table and referenced into the primary table, the name change would only have to be changed once in the separate table. Since that data is referenced into the primary table, any subsequent calls to the data would return the newly updated name and email reference.

So instead of having one big table with many fields of repeating data, you'd have two or three smaller tables. One table, the primary table with the news and articles, would have many rows of data, while the author name and email table would be fairly small, having only as many rows as you have authors.

It also makes sense to group together the information that you take out of the main table. Instead of creating separate tables each for the authors' names and email addresses, you could just include those two fields together in one separate table.

After rationalizing our primary table, it might look something like this:

```
+---------------+--------------+------+-----+---------+----------------+
| Field         | Type         | Null | Key | Default | Extra          |
+---------------+--------------+------+-----+---------+----------------+
| news_id       | int(11)      |      | PRI | 0       | auto_increment |
| heading       | varchar(48)  | YES  |     | NULL    |                |
| body          | text         | YES  |     | NULL    |                |
| date          | date         | YES  |     | NULL    |                |
| author        | int(11)      | YES  |     | NULL    |                |
+---------------+--------------+------+-----+---------+----------------+
```

The separate table for the authors' names and email addresses might look something like this:

```
+---------------+--------------+------+-----+---------+----------------+
| Field         | Type         | Null | Key | Default | Extra          |
+---------------+--------------+------+-----+---------+----------------+
| author_id     | int(11)      |      | PRI | 0       | auto_increment |
| author_name   | varchar(48)  | YES  |     | NULL    |                |
| author_email  | varchar(48)  | YES  |     | NULL    |                |
+---------------+--------------+------+-----+---------+----------------+
```

But exactly how is that referenced? you ask. In some relational databases there is the notion of a secondary key that automatically references the data in other tables. Unfortunately, MySQL doesn't have that feature at this time. Instead, you have to reference the separated data in your SQL statements.

In the `data_out.php3` script in Chapter 7, the SQL statement to select data from the primary table was written like this:

```
$sql = "select * from news order by 'date'";
$result = mysql_query($sql);
while ($row = mysql_fetch_array($result)) {
// Print out the Data
```

Now that you have created multiple tables, you need to do a little more to get all the data that you need out of the database. The statements below give an example of how this can be done.

```
$sql = "select * from news order by 'date'";
$result = mysql_query($sql);
while ($row = mysql_fetch_array($result)) {
 $author = $row["author"];
 $sql2 = "select * from authors where author_id = $author";
 $result2 = mysql_query($sql2);
 $row2 = mysql_fetch_array($result2);
 //Print the data
```

Notice that you now have to do two queries. You have to do one query for the *main* table, then another to get the author data, which is referenced in the data returned from the main query.

In the second set of code above, you would print out the fields from the *main* table by referencing the SQL data from the primary table as `$row["FIELD"]`. To print out the author information from the second table, you would need to reference the data as `$row2["FIELD"]`.

It's only necessary to select the data like the above example if you are trying to get everything out of the database. If you wanted to get just one record out of the database and you had the record ID, you could get the information out of the primary table and get the data in the referenced table at the same time by doing a query like this:

```
$sql = "select * from news, authors where news.news_id =
 '$id' and news.author = authors.author_id";
```

Whoa, what's going on with that? you might ask. If you are unfamiliar with SQL statements, then the code above may look a little strange. First, a plain English translation of the statement is, "Select everything from the news and authors tables, where the news_id field in the news table is `$id` and the author_id field in the authors table is the same as the author field in the news table." Second, you are going to need a book on SQL. SQL is a large language unto itself. It's bigger and more widespread than PHP, and is far beyond the scope of this book. Rest assured though, because I'll continue to explain the basics of SQL as they relate to the examples in this book.

There are a few basic principles to follow when creating SQL statements that access multiple tables. First, fire up the old MySQL command-line interface and make a few changes to the news table. Use the following three commands to delete the two columns associated with the author, and add a new column to reference a new author table.

```
mysql> ALTER TABLE news DROP author_name;
mysql> ALTER TABLE news DROP author_email;
mysql> ALTER TABLE news ADD author_id INT;
```

Now create the separate table for the authors.

```
mysql> CREATE TABLE authors (
    -> author_id INT NOT NULL AUTO_INCREMENT,
    -> author_name VARCHAR(32),
    -> author_email VARCHAR(64),
    -> PRIMARY KEY(author_id));
```

Now add an author into the newly created table.

```
mysql> INSERT INTO authors VALUES (NULL,
    -> 'Chris',
    -> 'chris@domain.com');
```

Now update the references in the news table to include the new author. Assume that the author whose name you enter has written all the articles.

```
mysql> update news set author_id = '1'
    -> where news_id > '0';
```

This references each article in the news table with an `author_id` of 1. This references to the author in the authors table who has the same author_id.

It's simple to get data from multiple tables. When you are building your SQL statement, you first have to mention which tables you want to access and separate the table names with a comma (,).

```
select * from news, authors;
```

The above command selects all of the data from both the news table and the authors table.

When you are accessing individual fields of multiple tables, the table name and a dot (.) must precede individual fields of a particular table. That means the fields in the news table can be referenced within an SQL statement like this:

- news.news_id
- news.heading
- news.body
- news.date
- news.author

The fields in the author table can be referenced within an SQL statement like this:

- `authors.author_id`
- `authors.author_name`
- `authors.author_email`

Once you have followed the basic principles, you can build your SQL statements just as you normally would.

Following are some examples of SQL statements using multiple tables.

```
select * from news, authors where
   author.author_name = 'Chris' and
   news.author_id = authors.author_id;
```

The above query selects all of the news items in the database that are written by the author Chris.

```
select * from news, authors where
   author.author_name = 'Chris' and
   news.author_id = authors.author_id and
   news.date = '2000-10-22';
```

The above query selects all of the news items in the database that are written by the author Chris and submitted on October 22, 2000.

```
select * from news, authors where
   author.author_name = 'Chris' and
   news.author_id = authors.author_id and
   news.heading like '%PHP%';
```

The above query selects all of the news items in the database that are written by the author Chris and that have a headline that includes the string *PHP*.

```
select * from news, authors where
   news.author_id = authors.author_id and
   news.body like '%PHP%';
```

The above query selects all of the items in the database that contain *PHP* in the body of the news. Note that in this example it wasn't necessary to access the authors table just to get the news items that contain PHP, but for completeness, the authors table is accessed so that the full data set for the record is retrieved from the database. This is useful if you are searching for only one item, but also want to print out associated information, such as the author's name, for the record.

I'd also like to add a note on date and time fields in a table. Although it is highly probable that you will have data rows in a table with the same date, and to a lesser extent the same time fields that have repeat data, I generally don't break these fields out into a separate table. I'm sure there are good arguments for doing such a thing, but I've never had the need to go through and change dates and times in a database used for things such as bulletin boards or news pages. However, if you are working with time-sensitive data, such as financial records, then it would probably behoove you to break these fields out into a separate table. In any case, be sure you use a four-digit number for the year. If there's anything to be learned from the events of the last few years, it's that you can never be too sure of how long your code may be around. Good coding practices now will help prevent a Y3K problem!

◆ User Authentication

PHP makes working with a database easy. You can add and delete data from a database through just about any Web browser. However, this also makes it easy for unauthorized people to go in and alter your database. The simple solution is to use some basic user authentication.

By basic, I mean really basic. The following methods work fine for everyday Web sites that don't contain sensitive data, like a community bulletin board or a small news site, but they aren't well suited for a database containing credit card numbers or your company's top secret blueprints for its latest processor design.

These methods should, however, keep the vast majority of people on the Internet from mucking about in your database.

First let's make a few changes to the existing authors table. You'll need a field for storing the passwords so that authors can post their news items to the database.

```
mysql> alter table authors ADD author_password VARCHAR(8);
```

The server responds with

```
Query OK, 1 row affected (0.00 sec)
Records: 1  Duplicates: 0  Warnings: 0
```

The authors table should now look like this:

```
mysql> describe authors;
+-----------------+-------------+------+-----+---------+----------------+
| Field           | Type        | Null | Key | Default | Extra          |
+-----------------+-------------+------+-----+---------+----------------+
| author_id       | int(11)     |      | PRI | 0       | auto_increment |
| author_name     | varchar(32) | YES  |     | NULL    |                |
| author_email    | varchar(64) | YES  |     | NULL    |                |
| author_password | varchar(8)  | YES  |     | NULL    |                |
+-----------------+-------------+------+-----+---------+----------------+
4 rows in set (0.06 sec
```

Now create a users table so that users of the site can post comments about a particular news item.

```
mysql> CREATE TABLE users (
    -> user_id INT NOT NULL AUTO_INCREMENT,
    -> user_name VARCHAR(32),
    -> user_email VARCHAR(64),
    -> user_password VARCHAR(8),
    -> PRIMARY KEY(user_id));
```

This table has exactly the same format as the authors table, with the exception of the names of the rows in the field column. Both the authors table and the users table will be used for user authentication.

Now, using the MySQL command line, add some data to the users table.

```
mysql> INSERT INTO users VALUES (
    -> NULL, 'Chris','Chris@someemail.com','password1');
```

Script 8-1 below can be used to check the password of a user. If the password is correct, the script returns a message that the password was accepted. If the password is incorrect, then the script returns a message that the password was wrong and re-prompts the user for his or her email address and password. Examples are shown in Figures 8–1, 8–2, 8–3, and 8–4.

Script 8-1
check_password.php3

```
1.  <html>
2.  <head>
3.     <title>Password Checking Script</title>
4.  </head>
5.  <body>
6.  <?php
7.  function print_form() {
8.     ?>
9.     <form action="check_password.php3" method="POST">
10.    <h3>Please Login</h3>
11.    User Name: <input type="text" name="user_name">
12.    <br>Password: <input type="password" name="password">
13.    <input type="submit" name="submit" value="Login!">
14.    </form>
15.    <?
16. }
17.
18. if(isset($submit)):
```

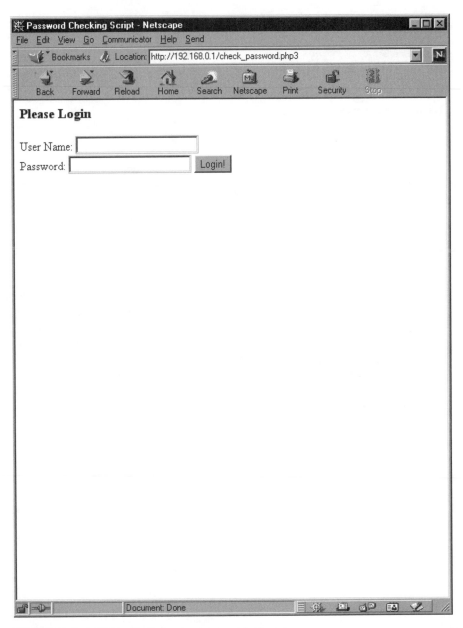

FIGURE 8–1 Initial load of check_password.hp3

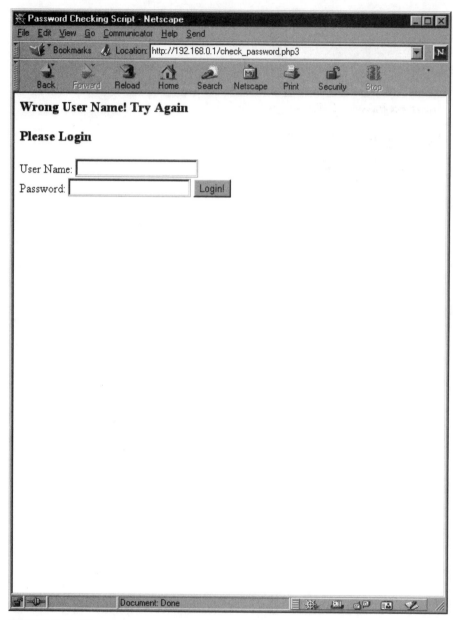

FIGURE 8–2 Wrong username entered

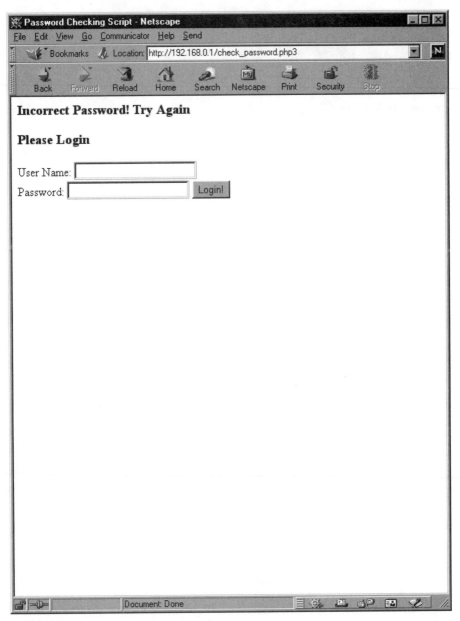

FIGURE 8-3 Wrong password entered

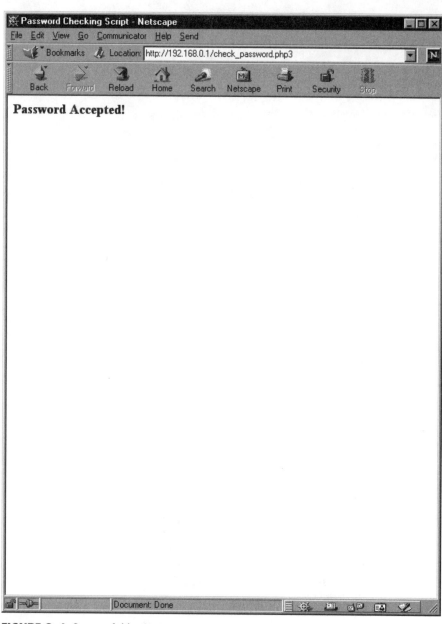

FIGURE 8-4 Successful login

```
19.    if(!$db = mysql_connect("localhost","root")):
20.          print("<h1>Can't Connect to the DB!</h1>\n");
21.    else:
22.          mysql_select_db("php3", $db);
23.    endif;
24.    $sql = "select * from users where user_name = '$user_name'";
25.    $result = mysql_query($sql);
26.    $row_count = mysql_num_rows($result);
27.    if($row_count == 0):
28.          ?>
29.          <h3>Wrong User Name! Try Again</h3>
30.          <?
31.          print_form();
32.    else:
33.    $row = mysql_fetch_array($result);
34.       if($password != $row["user_password"]):
35.          ?>
36.          <h3>Incorrect Password! Try Again</h3>
37.          <?
38.          print_form();
39.       else:
40.          ?>
41.          <h3>Password Accepted!</h3>
42.          <?
43.       endif;
44. endif;
45. else:
46. print_form();
47. endif;
48. ?>
49. </body>
50. </html>
```

HOW THE SCRIPT WORKS

- Lines 1 through 5 are normal HTML.
- Line 6 is the trusty PHP start tag. The Web server is now reading the page as PHP instead of as normal HTML.
- Lines 7 through 16 contain a function that simply prints out the login form to the page. This code is enclosed in a function because it may need to be called in several parts of the script.
- Line 18 checks to see if the Submit button was pressed in the form. If the Submit button was pressed, then you know that you can read the data that was entered into the form. If the Submit button was not pressed, then the script jumps all the way down to line 45.

- If the Submit button was pressed, then lines 19 through 23 attempt to connect to the MySQL server. If there is a problem connecting to the MySQL server, then an error message is printed out. If no errors are encountered while connecting to the database, then the script accesses the specified database.
- Lines 24 through 26 query the database and count the number of rows in the result set.
- Lines 27 through 31 check to see if any rows were returned from the SQL query. If no rows are returned, then the script assumes that the username is invalid because the script uses the username entered into the form as the basis for finding the correct row in the database. If no rows are returned, then the script prints out an error message telling the user that they entered an incorrect username, and the form is reprinted to the screen.
- At lines 32 through 38, the password is checked against the results of the query if there is a match in the database against the username. If the password entered into the form by the user does not match the password in the database, then an error message occurs and the form is printed to the screen.
- At lines 39 through 43, if the password is correct, then the user is notified that they entered a correct password and that access is granted. Usually at this point you would include the code or information that was password protected.
- Line 44 contains the `endif` for the `if/then/else` statement started on line 27.
- Lines 45 through 47 are executed if the Submit button has not been pressed. Basically, it assumes that this is the first time the user is viewing the page for a particular session and needs to enter his or her authentication information.
- Line 48 is the trusty close PHP tag. The Web server stops reading the page as PHP and begins reading it as normal HTML again.
- Lines 49 and 50 contain the normal HTML to close out the page.

◆ Project: Creating a Mini Slashdot for the *Stitch* Site

One of the more successful, if not the most successful Open Source news sites available on the Web is Slashdot at *http://www.slashdot.org*. The concept of Slashdot is simple—it provides news tidbits to its readers and allows them to add comments to each of the news articles that is posted. Readers get to add their two cents on the given subject, as well as provide more information about the story.

Slashdot has, of course, a bunch of other features that make it the great site that it is, but the basic premise of the site is fairly easy to code in PHP. This project teaches you how to create a mini Slashdot site of your own.

The example for this code is based on the fictional *Stitch Magazine's* new page.

To get started, let's create a new news table in the database and call it *news2*.

```
mysql> create table news2 (
    -> news_id INT NOT NULL AUTO_INCREMENT,
    -> title VARCHAR(32),
    -> intro TEXT,
    -> more TEXT,
    -> author_id INT,
    -> category_id INT,
    -> date DATE,
    -> time TIME,
    -> PRIMARY KEY(news_id));
```

The server should respond with something like

```
Query OK, 0 rows affected (0.05 sec)
```

Now you need to create a table in the database for users to add comments to each post.

```
mysql> create table comments (
    -> comment_id INT NOT NULL AUTO_INCREMENT,
    -> news_id INT,
    -> user_id INT,
    -> comment TEXT,
    -> PRIMARY KEY(comment_id));
```

The server should again respond with

```
Query OK, 0 rows affected (0.06 sec)
```

Finally, you need to create a table for the different categories for the news stories.

```
mysql> create table categories (
    -> category_id INT NOT NULL AUTO_INCREMENT,
    -> category VARCHAR(32),
    -> PRIMARY KEY(category_id));
```

Now insert some data into the categories.

```
mysql> insert into categories values (
    -> NULL, 'Fashion');
mysql> insert into categories values (
    -> NULL, 'Gossip');
```

You can reuse your existing tables for authors and users to do the user authentication for posting news items and comments, but you need to make one adjustment to the existing authors table. You need to give the author a password. You can do that with the following code at the MySQL command prompt:

```
mysql> update authors set author_password = 'password'
    -> where author_id = '1';
```

Code explanations appear immediately after each function or subsection of the script.

Examples are shown in Figures 8–5 through 8–9.

Script 8-2
stitchdot.php3

```
1.  <?php
2.  /* START FUNCTION DECS */
3.  function connect() {
4.      if(!$db = mysql_connect("localhost","root")):
5.              print("<h1>Can't Connect to the DB!</h1>\n");
6.      else:
7.                      mysql_select_db("php3", $db);
8.      endif;
9.      }
```

HOW THE SCRIPT WORKS

- Lines 1 and 2 merely contain the PHP start tag and a comment stating that some function declarations are being made.
- Line 3 is the function definition. The function name is simply connect and it takes no arguments. This function is used to connect to a MySQL database server.
- Line 4 attempts to connect to the MySQL database on the local host, using a username of "root" and no password. If the script cannot connect to the database (remember the "!" means NOT), then the code on line 5 is executed. Line 5 simply prints a brief error message to the screen, notifying the user that there is a problem.

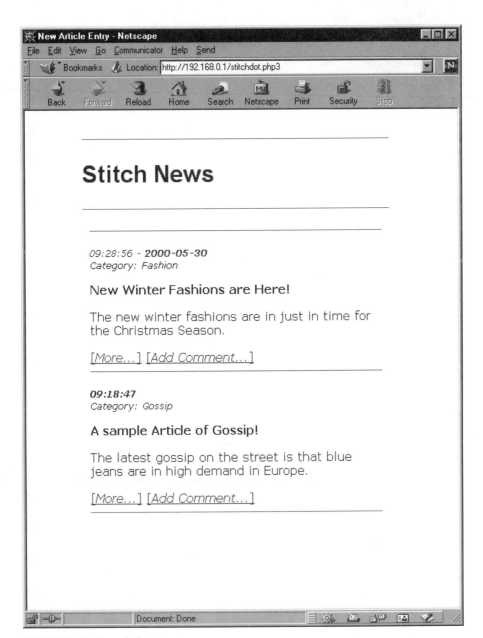

FIGURE 8-5 Sample front page

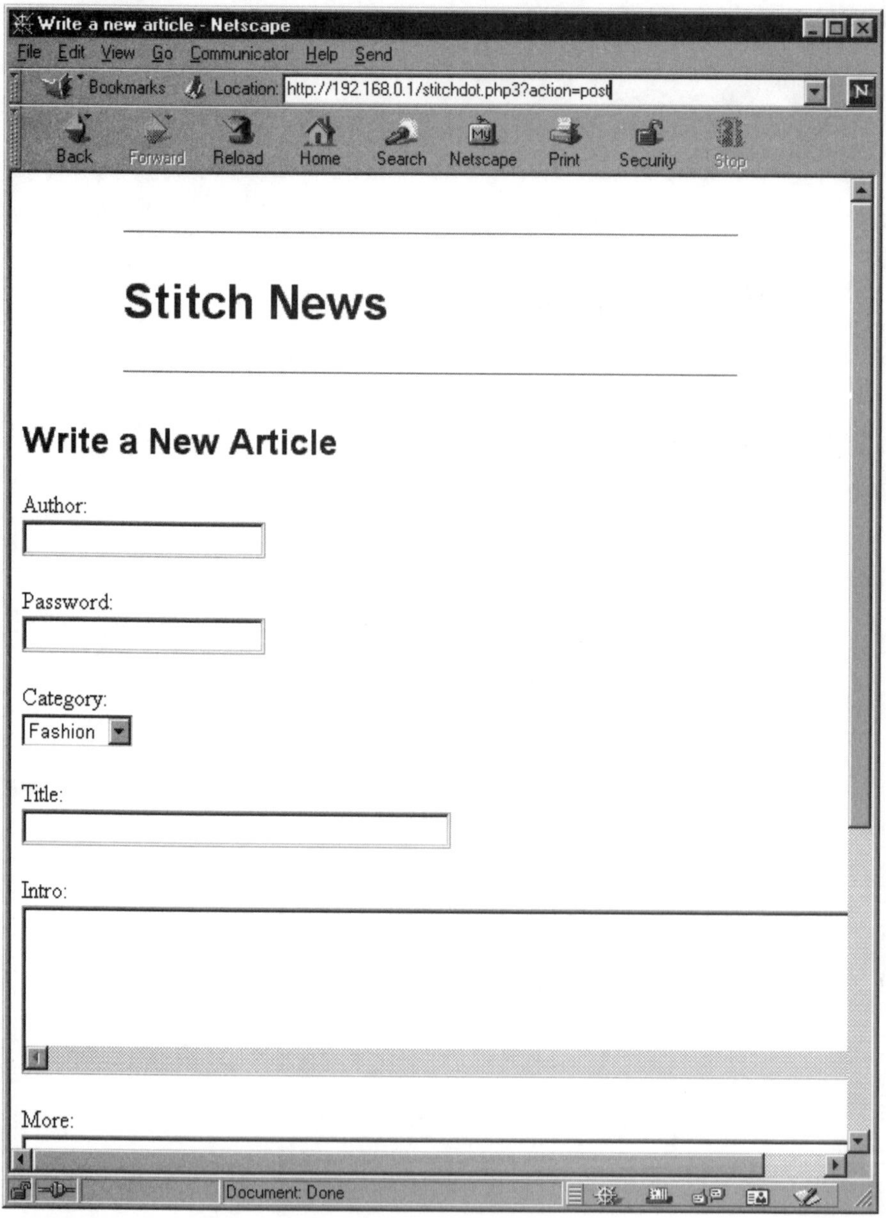

Stitch News

Write a New Article

Author:

Password:

Category:
Fashion

Title:

Intro:

More:

Document: Done

FIGURE 8–6 The Article Entry page

FIGURE 8-7 Wrong password when entering an article

FIGURE 8–8 A full article with comments

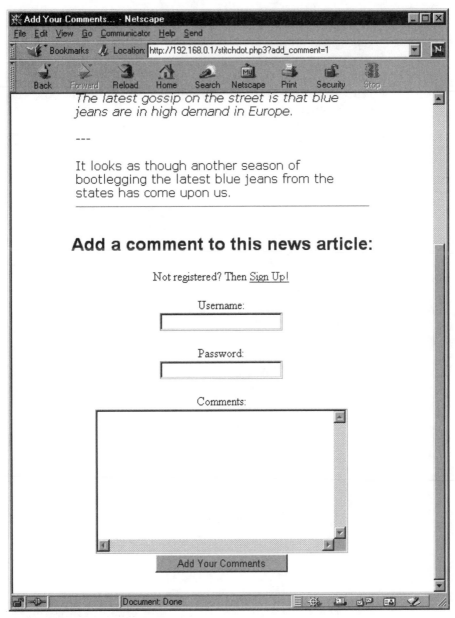

FIGURE 8–9 The Add Comments page

- At line 6, if the script is able to establish a connection to the database server, then the code in line 7 is executed. Line 7 selects the database on the server that the script will use for its subsequent database functions.
- Line 8 ends the `if/then/else` statement started on line 4.
- Line 9 contains the close curly brace, which denotes the end of this function.

```
10.  function head($title) {
11.    ?>
12.    <html>
13.    <head>
14.    <title><? echo $title ?></title>
15.    <meta http-equiv="Content-Type" content="text/html;
       charset=iso-8859-1">
16.    <style type="text/css">
17.    <!--
18.    BODY  {font-family : Verdana, Arial, Helvetica;}
19.    H1, H2, H3, H4, H5, H6   {font-family : Arial, Helvetica,
       Verdana, sans-serif;}
20.    TD  {font-family : Verdana, Arial, Helvetica;}
21.    PRE  {font-family : Courier Fixed;}
22.    .date  {
23.        font-size : small;
24.        font-family : Verdana;
25.        font-style : italic;
26.    }
27.    -->
28.    </style>
29.    </head>
30.    <body>
31.    <table width="420" border="0" align="CENTER">
32.    <tr><td> 
33.    <hr align="LEFT" size="1" width="420" noshade>
34.    <h1>Stitch News</h1>
35.    <hr align="LEFT" size="1" width="420" noshade>
36.    </td></tr>
37.    </table>
38.    <?
39.    }
```

- Line 10 contains the beginning of another function declaration. The function is called `head` and takes one argument, the `$title` variable. This function prints out the basic HTML found at the top of each page for the script. The `$title` variable can be used to give each page generated by the script a different title that appears in the title bar of the user's browser.

- Line 11 contains the close PHP tag. The function is almost entirely plain HTML, with the exception of line 14.
- Lines 12 and 13 are normal HTML tags.
- Line 14 is where the `$title` variable is used in this function. This allows for the page to have a dynamic title depending on what actions are going on within the script.
- Lines 15 through 37 are all normal HTML and should look familiar to you. Also notice that the STYLE tags are used to give the page a more polished look.
- Lines 38 and 39 move back into PHP with the close PHP tag and close the function with the close curly brace.

```
40.  function write_post(){
41.
42.     ?>
43.     <h2>Write a New Article</h2>
44.     <form action="stitchdot.php3" method="post">
45.     <p>Author: <br> <input type="text" name="author">
46.     <p>Password: <br><input type="password" name="password">
47.     <p>Category: <br><? catList(); ?>
48.     <p>Title:<br><input type="text" name="title" size="36"
   maxlength="36">
49.     <p>Intro:<br><textarea cols=75 rows=5
   name="intro"></textarea>
50.     <p>More:<br><textarea cols=75 rows=15
   name="more"></textarea>
51.
52.     <p><input type="submit" name="submit">
53.     </form>
54.     <?
55.  }
```

- Line 40 begins with a function declaration for the `write_post` function. This function prints out a form to the browser that allows authors to submit new articles to the site.
- Lines 42 through 46 escape from PHP and output the normal HTML that displays the form in the user's browser.
- Line 47 prints the output from the `catList` function, which is described below.
- Lines 48 through 53 print more of the form to the user's browser.
- Finally, lines 54 and 55 go back into PHP and close the function.

```
56.  function enter_post($author, $password, $title, $intro, $more,
   $category) {
57.     connect();
```

```
58.     $sql = "select * from authors where author_name =
        '$author'";
59.     $result = mysql_query($sql);
60.     $row = mysql_fetch_array($result);
61.     if($row["author_password"] != $password):
62.             print("<h1>Wrong Password!</h1>");
63.     else:
64.             $author = $row["author_id"];
65.             $time = date("H:i:s");
66.             $date = date("y-m-d");
67.             $sql = "insert into news2
        VALUES(NULL,'$title','$intro','$more','$author','$category',
        '$date','$time')";
68.             mysql_query($sql);
69.     endif;
70.     }
```

- Line 56 contains the function declaration for the `enter_post` function. The `enter_post` function takes the data that the user entered into the form from the `write_post` function and enters it all into the database. This function takes several arguments, all of which are fields from the `write_post` form.
- Line 57 calls the `connect` function to establish a connection to the database so that the script can store the data from the form.
- Line 58 creates an SQL statement that is used to check the author's name from the form against the author's name in the database.
- Line 59 sends the SQL query to the database and stores the results of the query in the variable `$result`. The query should return the author's information stored in the database. The key thing the script is going to look for is the result in the password field.
- Line 60 takes the `$result` and turns it into an array so that the script can check each field returned in the result. It calls this array `$row`.
- Line 61 checks to see if the password entered in the form `$password` is the same as the correct password in the database, `$row["author_password"]`. If the two passwords do not match, then line 62 prints out a message to the browser informing the user.
- Lines 63 through 66 are executed if the passwords match. Line 64 gets the numerical author ID from the previous query and stores it in the variable `$author`.

- Lines 65 and 66 generate some variables for the date and time that are inserted into the database to note the date and time the article was written.
- Line 67 contains the SQL statement that is used to actually store all of the new data in the database.
- Line 68 actually sends the SQL query to the server, resulting in the new data being stored.
- Line 69 closes the `if/then/else` statement started on line 61.
- And finally, line 70 closes out the function.

```
71. function display($show_what) {
72.    switch ($show_what) {
73.          case "":
74.             $sql = "select * from news2 where(TO_DAYS(NOW())-
    TO_DAYS(date)) <= '1' ORDER BY date DESC, time DESC";
75.             break;
76.          default:
77.             $sql = "select * from news2 where (TO_DAYS(NOW())-
    TO_DAYS(date)) <= '1' ORDER BY date DESC, time DESC";
78.             break;
79.    }
80.    display_posts($sql);
81.    }
```

- Line 71 contains the function declaration for the `display` function. The `display` function can be used to display different dates of articles on the main page of the site, or by default, the last two days worth of articles.
- Lines 72 through 79 contain the `switch` statement that is used to determine which SQL statement is used to generate the articles extracted from the database. Currently there are only two options, both of which are the same. Note that the SQL query orders the rows first by date, then by time, both in descending order (denoted by the DESC after the row names).
- Line 80 calls the `display_posts` function, described below, which actually prints out the posts.
- Line 81 closes the function.

```
82. function display_posts($sql) {
83.    connect();
84.    $result = mysql_query($sql);
85.    ?>
86.    <table width="400" border="0" cellpadding="5"
    align="CENTER">
87.    <tr><td>
```

```
88.    <hr align="RIGHT" size="1" width="400" noshade>
89.    </td></tr>
90.    <?
91.    while($row = mysql_fetch_array($result)) {
92.    ?>       <tr><td> <?
93.    if($last_date == $row["date"]):?>
94.    <p class="date"><b><?echo $row["time"]?></b>
95.    <?else:?>
96.    <p class="date"><?echo $row["time"]?> - <b><?echo
       $row["date"]?></b>
97.    <?endif;
98.    $cat_num = $row["category_id"];
99.    $cat_result = mysql_query("select categories.category from
       news2, categories where news2.category_id =
       categories.category_id and news2.category_id = '$cat_num'");
100.   $cat = mysql_fetch_array($cat_result);
101.   ?>
102.   <br>Category: <i><?echo $cat["category"] ?></i>
103.   <p><?echo "<b>".$row["title"]."</b>\n" ?>
104.   <p><?echo $row["intro"] ?><br>
105.   <?
106.   printf("\n<p><a  href=\"stitchdot.php3?more=%s\">
       [<i>More...</i>]</a>\n", $row["news_id"]);
107.   printf("\n <a href=\"stitchdot.php3?add_comment=%s\">[<i>Add
       Comment...</i>]</a>\n", $row["news_id"]);
108.   $last_date = $row["date"];
109.   ?>
110.   <hr align="RIGHT" size="1" width="400" noshade>
111.   </td></tr>
112.   <?
113.   }
114.   ?> </table> <?
115.   }
```

- Line 82 contains the function declaration for the display_
  posts function. It takes as its argument the SQL query generated in the show_what function.
- Line 83 calls the connect function because the script needs
  to access the data stored in the database to display the
  articles.
- Line 84 sends the SQL query that was given as the argument
  to this function to the server.
- Lines 85 through 90 print out HTML that sets up a table
  where the articles are displayed in the browser.
- Line 91 loops through all the rows returned in the query
  and turns them into an array so that the script can access
  the individual fields of data.

- Line 92 prints out a <TR> and <TD> tag. Each of the articles is printed out in one row of the table in the browser. The table doesn't have any borders, so it doesn't actually look like a table in the browser, but it allows you to have the page nicely laid out.
- Lines 93 through 97 may seem a little peculiar at first glance, but if you look at Figure 8–5 it may give you a better idea of what the code does. One of the ideas behind this site is that more than one article a day is posted, and on any given day you may have four or five articles. Additionally, you may want to display more than one day's worth of articles on the front page (by default, the script is set up to show two days of articles). Rather than print the date next to each article, only the latest entry for any given day shows the date. Any articles preceding the latest article that was posted on the same day will not show the date. With that said, these lines of code check to see if the date for the current row is the same as the date in the last row. If they are the same, the script prints the time and not the date. If the dates are different, then the date is printed, because obviously it's a new day.
- Line 98 through 100 select the `category_id` returned from the query and cross-reference it with the actual name in the categories table. Line 100 then grabs the row of information from the database.
- Lines 101 through 105 print out the Category, Title, and Introduction of the article.
- Line 106 prints out a link to the remainder of the article.
- Line 107 prints out a link that brings users to a page so that they may comment on an article.
- Line 108 ties in with lines 93 through 97. It sets the current date to the "last date," so that when the `while` loop is looped again, line 93 has something to check against to see if the dates are the same.
- Lines 109 through 112 print out a horizontal rule and print the HTML tags to close this row in the table.
- Line 113 is the end of the `while` loop started on line 91.
- Line 114 closes the table that displays the set of articles.
- Line 115 is the close curly brace which ends this function.

```
116.  function catList() {
117.      connect() ?>
118.      <select name="category">
119.      <?
```

```
120.            $sql = "select * from categories";
121.            $result = mysql_query($sql);
122.            while($row = mysql_fetch_array($result)) {
123.            printf("<option value=\"%s\">%s</option>",
      $row["category_id"], $row["category"]);
124.            }
125.    ?>
126.    </select>
127.    <?
128.    }
```

- Line 116 contains the function declaration for the `catList` function. This function takes no arguments. This is actually just a simple little function that loops through one table in the database and creates an HTML select list of the values in the table. When it's done running, it gives you a nice pull-down menu of all the categories that one can classify an article under. Of course, you have to enter the categories into the categories table first!
- Line 117 calls the `connect` function to connect to the database.
- Line 118 prints out the HTML code to begin displaying a pull-down menu in the browser.
- Lines 119 through 124 connect to the database, select everything from the categories table, and print out the values to the browser, enclosing the values in the proper HTML tags so they are correctly displayed.
- Lines 125 through 127 pop out of PHP to print the HTML `close select` tag.
- Line 128 ends the function declaration for this function.

```
129.  function more($more) {
130.          connect();
131.          $sql = "select * from news2 where news_id =
      '$more'";
132.          $result = mysql_query($sql);
133.          $row = mysql_fetch_array($result);
134.          ?>
135.          <table width="400" border="0" cellpadding="5"
      align="CENTER">
136.          <tr><td>
137.          <hr align="RIGHT" size="1" width="400" noshade>
138.          <p class="date"><?echo $row["time"]?> - <b><?echo
      $row["date"]?></b>
139.          <?
140.          $cat_num = $row["category_id"];
```

```
141.            $cat_result = mysql_query("select
       categories.category from news2, categories where
       news2.category_id = categories.category_id and
       news2.category_id = '$cat_num'");
142.            $cat = mysql_fetch_array($cat_result);
143.            ?>
144.            <br>Category: <i><?echo $cat["category"] ?></i>
145.            <p><?echo "<b>".$row["title"]."</b>" ?>
146.            <p><?echo "<i>" . $row["intro"] . "</i>"?>
147.            <p><?echo "---<p>" . $row["more"] ?>
148.            <hr align="RIGHT" size="1" width="400" noshade>
149.            </tr></td>
150.            </table>
151.            <?
152.            }
```

- Line 129 contains the function declaration for the `more` function. This function takes as its argument the ID of an article.
- Line 130 calls the `connect` function that allows the script to connect to the database.
- Lines 131 through 133 query the database for the proper article, referenced by the ID that was passed to the function, and put the results of the query into an array.
- Lines 134 through 137 print out the HTML code for layout of the table that the article is displayed in.
- Line 138 prints out the time and date the article was written.
- Lines 139 through 144 fetch the cross-referenced category name from the categories table.
- Lines 145 through 147 print out the article in its entirety. The introduction of the article is printed in italics because it's assumed that the reader has already read the introduction on the main page, and can now just go down and read the rest of the article.
- Lines 148 through 151 print out the HTML tags that close out the table.
- Line 152 is the close curly brace, which denotes the end of this function.

```
153. function show_comments($id) {
154.            $sql = "select * from comments where news_id =
       '$id'";
155.            $result = mysql_query($sql);
156.            $cnt = mysql_num_rows($result);
157.            print("<center><P><b>There are $cnt comments for
       this post.</b><P></center>\n");
```

```
158.            if($cnt > '0'):
159.                ?>
160.                <table width="390" border="1" cellspacing="0"
       cellpadding="5" align="CENTER">
161.                <?
162.                while($row = mysql_fetch_array($result)){
163.                $user_id = $row["user_id"];
164.    $sql2 = "select * from users where user_id =
       '$user_id'";
165.                $result2 = mysql_query($sql2);
166.                $row2 = mysql_fetch_array($result2);
167.                $comments = stripslashes($row["comment"]);
168.                printf("<tr><td><i>Comment by
       %s:</i><br><PRE>%s</PRE></tr></td>", $row2["user_name"],
       $comments);
169.                    }
170.                ?>
171.                <tr><td>
172.                <?
173.                printf("\n <a href=\"stitchdot.php3?
       add_comment=%s\">[<i>Add Comment...</i>]</a>\n", $id);
174.                ?>
175.                </td></tr>
176.                </table>
177.                <?
178.            endif;
179.            }
```

- Line 153 contains the function declaration for the show_com-ments function, which takes as an argument the ID of an article. This function is called if a user wishes to see any comments that other users may have left for a particular article.
- Lines 154 and 155 query the database for any comments linked to a particular article's ID.
- Line 156 counts the number of comments linked to the article ID.
- Line 157 prints out a sentence to the browser stating how many comments have been posted regarding the particular article.
- At line 158, if there are comments (more than zero), then the following lines are executed. If there are no comments, then the script goes directly to line 178.
- Lines 159 through 161 print out the HTML code for the beginning of the table that holds the comments.

- If there are comments then the `while` statement in line 162 begins to loop through the results of the query in lines 154 and 155, and puts the results into an array.
- Lines 163 through 166 take the ID of the user who posted the comment and cross-reference it with the user's actual name.
- Line 167 escapes any slashes that the user may have put in their comments so that it doesn't interfere with the HTML code on the page.
- Lines 168 through 172 print out the user's name and comments, then close the row.
- Line 173 prints one last row in the table that has a link for users to add more comments.
- Lines 174 through 177 print out the HTML code that closes the table.
- Line 178 ends the `if/then` statement started on line 158.
- Finally, line 179 contains the close curly brace, which ends this function.

```
180.   function add_comment ($id) {
181.              ?>
182.              <center>
183.              <form action="stitchdot.php3" method="POST">
184.              <h2>Add a comment to this news article:</h2>
185.              <P>Not registered? Then <a href="stitchdot.php3?
       signup=newuser">Sign Up!</a>
186.              <input type="hidden" name="news_id" value="<? echo
       $id ?>">
187.              <p>Username: <br><input type="text"
       name="user_name">
188.              <p>Password: <br><input type="password"
       name="password">
189.              <p>Comments: <br><textarea cols=40 rows=10
       name="comments"></textarea>
190.              <br><input type="submit" name="insert_comments"
       value="Add Your Comments">
191.              </form>
192.              </center>
193.              <?
194.              }
```

- Line 180 contains the function declaration for the `add_com-ment` function. It takes as an argument the ID of a particular article.

- Lines 181 through 193 print out an HTML form for the users to enter any comments they have on any article. Basically, it asks for the user's username and password and provides an HTML text area for he or she to enter comments. If the user does not have a username or password, then he or she can click on a link that brings the user to a page where he or she can sign up for one.
- Line 194 contains the close curly brace, closing this function.

```
195.    function insert_comments ($news_id, $user_name, $password,
        $comments) {
196.        connect();
197.        $sql = "select * from users where user_name =
        '$user_name'";
198.        $result = mysql_query($sql);
199.        $row_count = mysql_num_rows($result);
200.        if($row_count == 0):
201.            ?>
202.            <h3>Wrong User Name! Click the browsers Back
        Button and Try Again.</h3>
203.            <?
204.        else:
205.            $row = mysql_fetch_array($result);
206.            if($password != $row["user_password"]):
207.            ?>
208.            <h3>Incorrect Password! Click the browsers
        Back Button and Try Again.</h3>
209.            <?
210.            else:
211.            ?>
212.            <center><h3>Thanks for your
        comments!</h3></center>
213.            <?
214.            $user_id = $row["user_id"];
215.            $comments = addslashes($comments);
216.            $sql2 = "insert into comments values (NULL,
        '$news_id','$user_id','$comments')";
217.            mysql_query($sql2);
218.            more($news_id);
219.            show_comments($news_id);
220.            endif;
221.        endif;
222.    }
```

- Line 195 contains the function declaration for the insert_ comment function. It takes as its argument the ID of a particular article, the user's username and password, and the user's comments. This function basically takes the user input from the form generated by the `add_comment` function, checks to see if the user's password is correct, then enters the comments into the database.

- Line 196 calls the `connect` function, which connects the script to the database.
- Lines 197 through 199 generate an SQL query that checks to see if the user entered a valid username.
- Line 200 counts the number of rows returned from the query and checks to see if it returned zero.
- If it does return zero, then at lines 201 through 203 the script knows that the username does not exist in the user table and that it is not a valid username. A message is printed out informing the user of the error.
- If the username does exist in the database, then at lines 204 through 207 the script goes on to check if the password matches the same password for that user in the database.
- At lines 208 and 209, if the passwords do not match, then a message is printed to the screen informing the user of his or her error.
- If the password is correct, then at lines 210 through 220 a message is printed to the screen, thanking the user for his or her comments, and the proper SQL is generated to enter the comments into the database.
- Line 221 ends the `if/then/else` statement started on line 200.
- Line 222 contains the close curly brace that ends this function.

```
223.    function signup($signup, $user_name, $user_email,
        $user_password) {
224.            if($signup == "enter_user"):
225.                    connect();
226.                    $sql = "insert into users values (NULL,
        '$user_name', '$user_email', '$user_password')";
227.                    mysql_query($sql);
228.                    print("<h2>Thanks for Signing Up!</h2>");
229.            else:
230.            ?>
231.            <p>Please fill out this short registration form to
        add comments to our news articles:
232.            <form action="stitchdot.php3?signup=enter_user"
        method="POST">
233.            <input type="hidden" name="signup" value=
        "enter_user">
```

```
234.              <P>User Name: <input type="text" name="user_name">
235.              <br>Email: <input type="text" name="user_email">
236.              <br>Password: <input type="password"
      name="user_password" size="8" maxlength="8">
237.              <p><input type="submit" name="newuser" value=
      "Signup!">
238.              </form>
239.              <?
240.              endif;
241. }
242. /* END FUNCTION DECS */
243.
```

- Line 223 contains the function declaration for the `signup` function. It takes as its arguments a `$signup` variable and the user's name, email, and password. This function does two things: it prints out the form asking the user for his or her "Signing Up" information, and it enters that information into the database. It decides what action to take by the value of the `$signup` variable. If the `$signup` variable equals `newuser`, then it prints the form. If the `$signup` variable equals `enter_user`, then it enters the user into the database.

- Lines 224 through 228 check to see what the value of the `$signup` variable is. If it's `enter_user`, then the script calls the `connect` function and enters a query to add the user's information to the database. If it's not `enter_user`, then the script skips to line 229.

- Lines 229 through 240 print out the form asking a new user to create a login and password. Note the hidden variable for `signup`. This tells the script that the user has entered his or her information and the function should now enter that information into the database.

- Line 241 contains the close curly brace, denoting the end of this function.

```
244.    /* START MAIN PROGRAM */
245.    if(isset($submit)):
246.         head("New Article Entry");
247.         enter_post($author, $password, $title, $intro,
      $more, $category);
248.         display($show_what);
249.    elseif(isset($more)):
250.         head("More of the story...");
251.         more($more);
252.       show_comments($more);
253.    elseif(isset($add_comment)):
254.         head("Add Your Comments...");
```

```
255.            more($add_comment);
256.            add_comment($add_comment);
257.   elseif(isset($insert_comments)):
258.            head("Thanks for your comments!");
259.            insert_comments($news_id, $user_name, $password,
       $comments);
260.   elseif(isset($signup)):
261.            head("Signup to Post Comments");
262.            signup($signup, $user_name, $user_email,
       $user_password);
263.   elseif($action == "post"):
264.            head("Write a new article");
265.            write_post();
266.   else:
267.            head("Stitch Magazine News Stories");
268.            display($show_what);
269.   endif;
270.   /* END MAIN PROGRAM */
271.   ?>
272.   </body>
273.   </html>
```

- Now, finally, (drum roll, please) we come to the part of the script that ties everything together. Line 244 is merely a comment that states, "Start Main Program," meaning that everything up until this point has been functions, which aren't very useful by themselves. The following part of the script ties and glues all these functions together to make a nice little Web application.
- Lines 245 through 248 first check to see if the $submit variable is set. If the $submit variable is set, then the script knows that a user has pressed the Submit button on the article entry page. It then calls the head function, with an argument of "New Article Entry," (which is the page title), then calls the enter_post function to add the new article into the database, and finally calls the display function to print out the new article (along with preceding articles) to the page.
- Lines 249 through 252 are executed if the $more variable is set. If the $more variable is set, then the script knows that the user has clicked on a More link. The head function is called with an argument of More of the story…, then the more function is called with the ID of the article that is being displayed, and finally, the show_comments function is called to show any comments the user may have added to the article.
- At lines 253 through 256, if the $add_comment variable is set, then the script knows that the user has clicked on a link to

add a comment to a particular article. The `head` function is then called with an argument of `Add Your Comments...`, the `more` function is called to show the entire article, and finally, the `add_comment` function is called so that the user may add comments.

- If the `$insert_comments` variable is set, then at lines 257 through 259 the script knows that a user has entered his or her comments into the proper form. The `head` function is called with an argument of `Thanks for your comments!`, and the `insert_comments` function is called to enter in the user's comments.

- If the `$signup` variable is set, then at lines 260 through 262 the script knows that it needs to call the `signup` function.

- At lines 263 through 265 if the `$action` variable is set to post, then the script calls the `write_post` function, which prints the form out so an author can enter a new article into the database.

- If none of the variables are set, then at lines 266 through 269 the script merely prints out the basic page showing the articles defined by the `$show_what` variable.

- Lines 270 through 273 close out the main program's `if/then/else` structure, close out the PHP part of the script, and close out the HTML for the page.

◆ Recap

This chapter has hopefully shown you just how powerful PHP and MySQL can be. In only about 300 lines, you can write a fairly feature-rich and robust Web application. If you practice using multiple tables for your MySQL-based applications, and work on building your own functions for various tasks, you'll be building feature-rich Web applications in no time.

◆ Advanced Project

To keep the project fairly simple, some corners have been cut. Things such as checking to make sure entries were correctly inserted into the database were left out of Script 8-2. Also, the script doesn't provide a way for authors to add new categories. Currently, the only way to add a category is to do it from the MySQL command line. Go through the script and add the features that are lacking. Also, play around with the style sheet to get a look and feel that is right for your site.

9 PHP and MySQL References

◆ HTML Editors that Play Nice with PHP

One of the nice things about PHP, and about scripting languages in general, is that you don't need some bloated and expensive programming suite to create your Web applications. Any five-cent text editor works just fine. But there are a few applications out there that make programming PHP, and Web site management in general, easier and more convenient. During my escapades with PHP, I've come across three Web-editing applications that I have found to "play nice" with PHP. That is, they don't go through and try to mangle your code to fit some proprietary standard for creating Web pages. These applications are

- Allaire HomeSite 4.5
- Macromedia Dreamweaver 3
- VIM—Visual Editor Improved

Allaire HomeSite 4.5

HomeSite 4.5 is a great application for Web developers who have to use multiple Web technologies in their projects. The primary view of your projects is in text mode (as opposed to WYSIWYG).

HomeSite also has the excellent feature of color-coding PHP tags as shown in Figure 9–1. This feature makes reading your PHP code extremely easy, and also helps to remind you to close those quotes and comments.

Another really great feature of HomeSite is its ability to map a Web server to its browse window. Normally, if you looked at

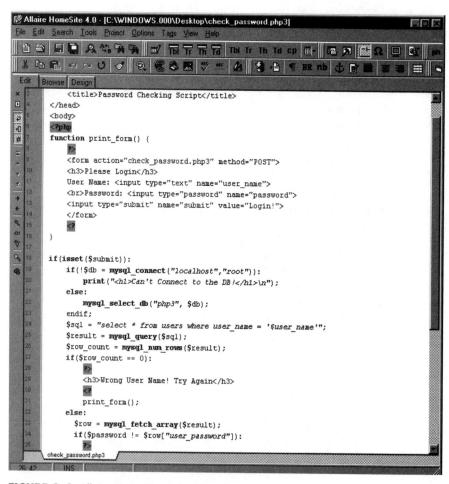

FIGURE 9–1 Allaire HomeSite 4.5 with color-coded PHP

PHP-enriched HTML using the browse or preview mode of an HTML editor, you'd see garbage. There might be some legible HTML, but there would be a lot of PHP snippets in there as well. None of the PHP content is being rendered correctly because it's all server-side generated. The preview modes of most HTML editors are strictly client-side.

The mapping actually lets you run any of your pages through a local Web server and display the output right from within HomeSite. Your PHP code is run through the Web server and displayed correctly within the editor.

You can get an evaluation version of HomeSite from Allaire's Web site at *http://www.allaire.com.*

Macromedia Dreamweaver 3

Dreamweaver 3 is more of a WYSIWYG HTML editing tool, but it is extremely useful for doing page layout and site management. It also has the feature of launching an external editor (such as HomeSite) to edit HTML and PHP markup. You can also edit the code directly from inside Dreamweaver, but the PHP code is not color-coded. An example of a page in Dreamweaver is shown in Figure 9–2.

You can download a free evaluation version of Dreamweaver from Macromedia's Web site at *http://www.macromedia.com.*

Macromedia and HomeSite Together

Another great thing about both HomeSite and Dreamweaver is their ability to work together. Both can be set up to switch almost seamlessly between the two applications. Doing some extensive work on some complicated tables? It's probably easier to use Dreamweaver. Want to switch over and edit some PHP on the same page in HomeSite? You can do it with the push of a button. And for the most part, neither application mangles the other's code.

VIM

Last but not least is the venerable VIM editor. VIM provides a nice Linux-based editor for PHP, and is an improved and expanded version of the classic UNIX-based vi editor. There are also versions of VIM for just about every operating system on the planet! You can download a free version of VIM from *www.vim.org.*

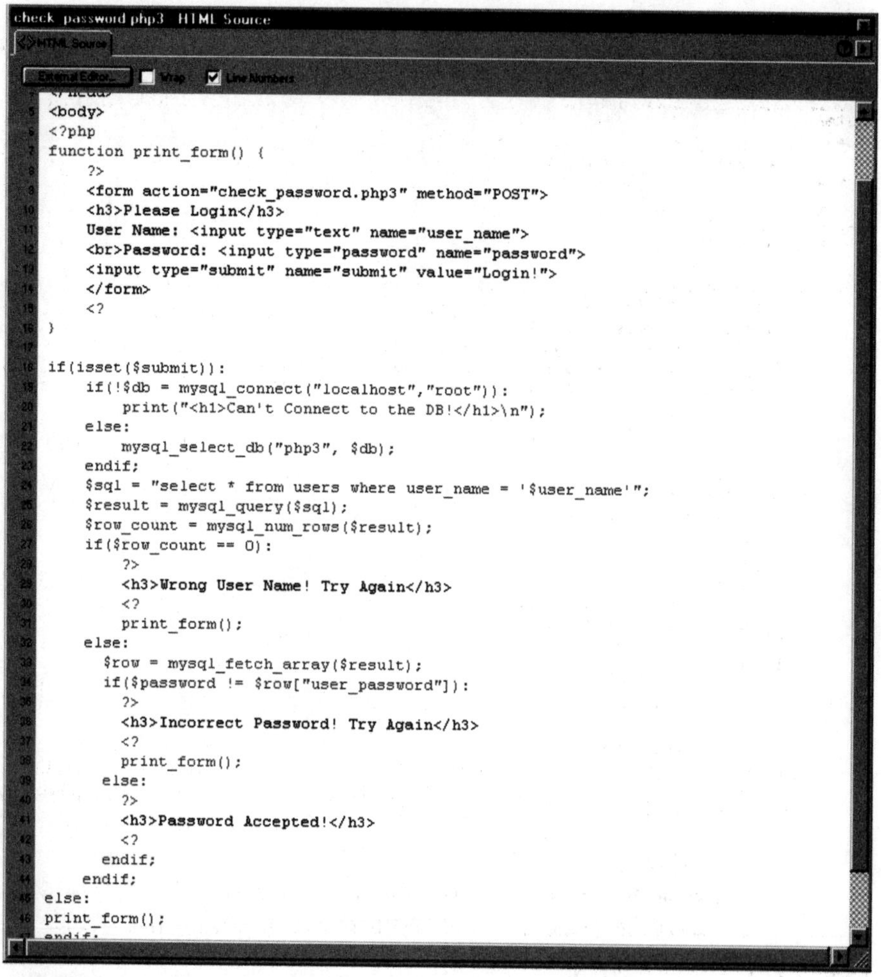

```
check_password.php3 HTML Source
<?HTML Source
External Editor...    Wrap    Line Numbers
</head>
<body>
<?php
function print_form() {
    ?>
    <form action="check_password.php3" method="POST">
    <h3>Please Login</h3>
    User Name: <input type="text" name="user_name">
    <br>Password: <input type="password" name="password">
    <input type="submit" name="submit" value="Login!">
    </form>
    <?
}

if(isset($submit)):
    if(!$db = mysql_connect("localhost","root")):
        print("<h1>Can't Connect to the DB!</h1>\n");
    else:
        mysql_select_db("php3", $db);
    endif;
    $sql = "select * from users where user_name = '$user_name'";
    $result = mysql_query($sql);
    $row_count = mysql_num_rows($result);
    if($row_count == 0):
        ?>
        <h3>Wrong User Name! Try Again</h3>
        <?
        print_form();
    else:
      $row = mysql_fetch_array($result);
      if($password != $row["user_password"]):
        ?>
        <h3>Incorrect Password! Try Again</h3>
        <?
        print_form();
      else:
        ?>
        <h3>Password Accepted!</h3>
        <?
      endif;
    endif;
else:
print_form();
endif;
```

FIGURE 9–2 Macromedia Dreamweaver 3 in source view

◆ Finding Help

There are literally hundreds of ways to get help with your PHP coding woes. There are mailing lists, online knowledge bases, Internet Relay Chats (IRCs), Web-based tutorials, and more. If you can't find help in one place, then you'll surely find it in another.

The best place to start out if you need some help is to look at the PHP support page located at *http://www.php.net/support.php3*.

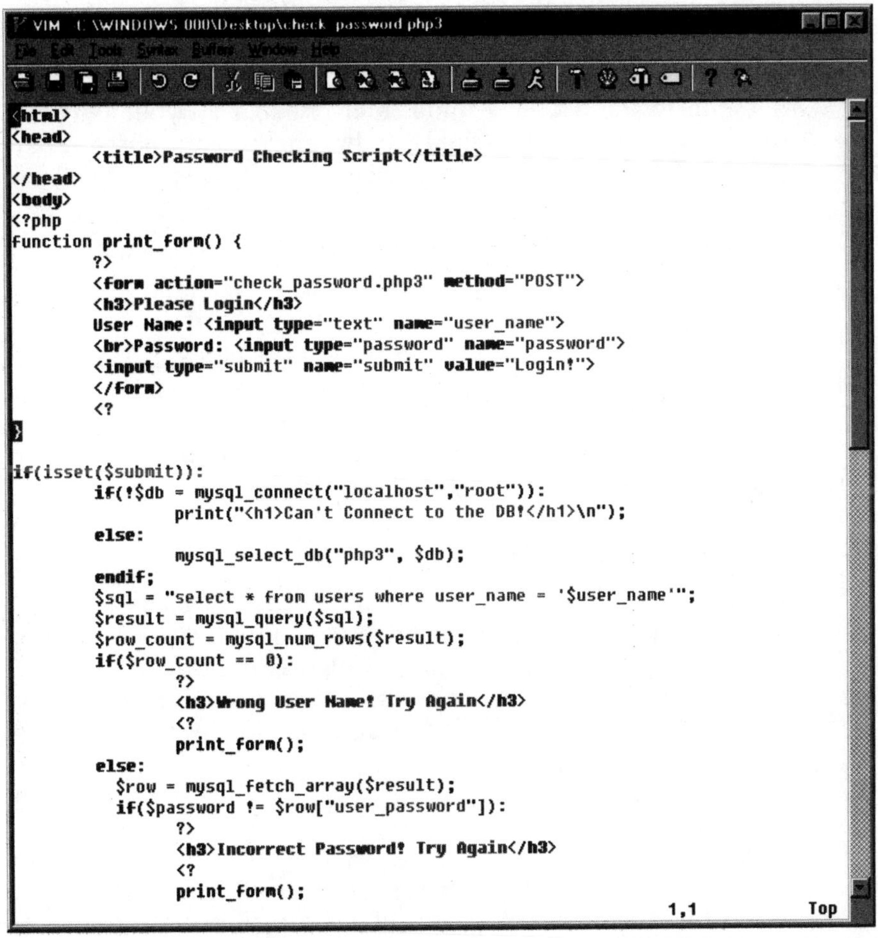

```
VIM  C:\WINDOWS\000\Desktop\check_password.php3                    [_][□][X]
File  Edit  Tools  Syntax  Buffers  Window  Help

<html>
<head>
        <title>Password Checking Script</title>
</head>
<body>
<?php
function print_form() {
        ?>
        <form action="check_password.php3" method="POST">
        <h3>Please Login</h3>
        User Name: <input type="text" name="user_name">
        <br>Password: <input type="password" name="password">
        <input type="submit" name="submit" value="Login!">
        </form>
        <?
}

if(isset($submit)):
        if(!$db = mysql_connect("localhost","root")):
                print("<h1>Can't Connect to the DB!</h1>\n");
        else:
                mysql_select_db("php3", $db);
        endif;
        $sql = "select * from users where user_name = '$user_name'";
        $result = mysql_query($sql);
        $row_count = mysql_num_rows($result);
        if($row_count == 0):
                ?>
                <h3>Wrong User Name! Try Again</h3>
                <?
                print_form();
        else:
          $row = mysql_fetch_array($result);
          if($password != $row["user_password"]):
                ?>
                <h3>Incorrect Password! Try Again</h3>
                <?
                print_form();
                                                        1,1        Top
```

FIGURE 9-3 VIM in Windows 98

The page provides a list of the more common places to find help and examples about PHP in general. Listed below are some of these places.

The PHP Mailing List

The PHP mailing list is a very active and helpful mailing list of PHP coders. But be forewarned, the list is *very* active. Currently the list receives over 100 email messages a day, ranging from common to obscure topics. If you have a PHP question, the chances are good that someone on the list can answer it. However, you should always do a little research on your own from some of the other resources mentioned below before you post a question to the list. Five minutes of research on your part will save a lot of people's time and bandwidth. You can subscribe to a variety of PHP mailing lists at *http://www.php.net/support.php3*.

Mailing List Archives

The questions you have about PHP have probably already been answered at one time or another on the PHP mailing list, especially if you are new to PHP. A good place to start is to check the general mailing list archives available at *http://marc .theaimsgroup.com/?l=php3-general*.

Other archives for some of the PHP mailing lists are also available from the PHP support page mentioned above.

PHP Knowledge Base

There is an excellent knowledge base at *http://php.faqts.com*. Information is categorized logically and is in a Question and Answer format. If your particular question is not answered in the knowledge base, you can pose it to the community. Many questions from the mailing list have also been archived here in an easily accessible manner.

phpbuilder.com

Another great Web-based resource for PHP tips and tricks, as well as for full-length tutorials and how-to's, is *http://www.phpbuilder .com*. The site has many excellent articles by hard-core programmers who really know their stuff.

Zend Technologies

Zend Technologies is the creator of Zend, the PHP4 engine. Their homepage provides many useful PHP4 resources, as well as some resources for PHP3. See *http://www.zend.com*.

◆ MySQL Function List

Below are some of the basic yet useful MySQL functions used in PHP, along with short code examples.

mysql_connect

You usually have to use this function, along with `mysql_select_db`, before you can do any type of queries on a database. The connection created by this function is usually assigned to a variable so that it can be referenced by other PHP MySQL functions.

```
$link = mysql_connect("HOSTNAME","USERNAME","PASSWORD")
```

mysql_select_db

This function lets you select a particular database on a MySQL server. You must first connect to the server using `mysql_connect`. It is equivalent to the `use DBNAME;` MySQL command-line command.

```
mysql_select_db("Database_Name", $link)
```

mysql_query

The nuts and bolts of dealing with a MySQL database is sending queries to it. You can't live without this function. Essentially, it lets you run any MySQL command you want to run on the database.

```
$result = mysql_query("SQL STATEMENT")
```

mysql_fetch_array

This function lets you take the data from a query and turn it into an array. Each element in the array is each field returned in the query.

```
$row = mysql_fetch_array("Result Of an SQL Query")
```

mysql_num_rows

This function counts the number of rows returned from a query and puts that value into a variable. It is useful for seeing just how many rows of data are returned in a query.

```
$number = mysql_num_rows("Result of an SQL Query")
```

mysql_num_fields

This function counts the number of fields returned from a query and puts that value into a variable.

```
$number = mysql_num_fields("Result of an SQL Query")
```

mysql_list_dbs

Got a server with a bunch of databases on it? Want to see the names of them all? This command lists all of the databases on a MySQL server.

```
$database_list_raw = mysql_list_dbs($link)
while ($row = mysql_fetch_array($database_list_raw)) {
printf("%s<br>", $row["databases"]; }
```

mysql_list_tables

This function is the same as above, only with tables in a particular database. You specify which server and database, and the following script returns the names of all the tables in that database.

```
$table_list_raw = mysql_list_tables("Database Name", $link)
while ($row = mysql_fetch_array($table_list_raw)) {
printf("%s<br>", $row["tables"]; }
```

mysql_list_fields

This function is the same as above, only with fields in a particular table. You specify server, database, and table name, and this script returns the names of the fields.

```
$fields_list_raw = mysql_list_fields("Database Name", "Table
  Name", $link)
while ($row = mysql_fetch_array($fields_list_raw)) {
printf("%s<br>", $row["fields"]; })
```

mysql_insert_id

This function gets the ID of the last row affected by the INSERT SQL Query. It is useful when you want to immediately return results from a table that just had data inserted into it, and use a function that queries on a table's ID.

```
$result = mysql_query("INSERT INTO table VALUES(…)");
$new_row_id = musql_insert_id();
```

As always, the complete list of MySQL functions with associated examples and annotations by users is available online. Go to *http://www.php.net/manual/ref.mysql.php.*

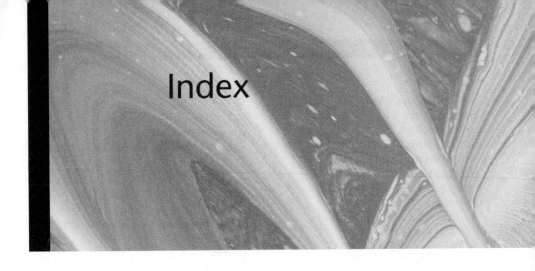

Index

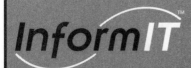